TRACING YOUR PAUPER ANCESTORS

TRACING YOUR PAUPER ANCESTORS

A Guide for Family Historians

ROBERT BURLISON

Pen & Sword
FAMILY HISTORY

First published in Great Britain in 2009 by
PEN & SWORD FAMILY HISTORY
an imprint of
Pen & Sword Books Ltd
47 Church Street
Barnsley
South Yorkshire
S70 2AS

ISBN 978 1 84415 985 7

The right of Robert Burlison to be identified as author of
this Work has been asserted by him in accordance with
the Copyright, Designs and Patents Act 1988.

Hertfordshire Libraries	
H45 787 583 9	
Askews	22-Oct-2009
929.1072	£12.99

Printed and bound in England by
CPI UK

Pen & Sword Books Ltd incorporates the Imprints of
Pen & Sword Aviation, Pen & Sword Family History, Pen & Sword Maritime,
Pen & Sword Military, Wharncliffe Local History, Pen & Sword Select,
Pen & Sword Military Classics, Leo Cooper, Remember When,
Seaforth Publishing and Frontline Publishing

For a complete list of Pen & Sword titles please contact
PEN & SWORD BOOKS LIMITED
47 Church Street, Barnsley, South Yorkshire, S70 2AS, England
E-mail: enquiries@pen-and-sword.co.uk
www.pen-and-sword.co.uk

CONTENTS

Dedicated to
Robert James Burlison
1920–1984

'Pauperism was a status, entry to which affected not merely a part of a man's life, but the whole of it. He became a pauper for all purposes and he carried his family with him. Paupers formed a distinct group of second class citizens, deprived of the most important rights of citizenship; firstly the loss of personal reputation, secondly, the loss of personal freedom and, thirdly, the loss of political freedom by suffering disenfranchisement.'

T H Marshall, *Social Policy*, 1965

PREFACE

Poverty has affected a large mass of the population throughout the centuries. There are few of us who will not have an ancestor, or a branch of the family, who had fallen on hard times or were in some way touched by destitution. It has been estimated that 80 per cent of the population have some direct or indirect past family connection with poverty. Perhaps an ancestor was a wandering vagrant; a recipient of poor-relief or charity aid; an inmate in a workhouse; or, in some other way was affected by the decision of a Poor Law official. Then there were those who, although not poor themselves, supplied a workhouse with goods or services; or worked there; or served as an overseer to the poor, on a Board of Governors or as a trustee of a charity established to help the poor. Yet little has been written in recent years with the family historian in mind on the causes and effects of poverty, how it was perceived and how it was relieved (or not) through the work of individuals, the support of charities and the intervention of the state. This book attempts to redress the balance.

It adopts poverty as its principle theme and explores how charitable relief in its many forms played an important part in addressing the needs of the poor. From monastic beginnings, individuals and organisations displaying pastoral care, religious fervour or philanthropic ideals brought the plight of the destitute and their grinding poverty to the attention of a wider audience. This created, or awakened, a social conscience that helped the least fortunate of society and was instrumental in the founding principles of charities whose objects were (or are) the relief of the poor.

The largely repressive Poor Laws are also discussed in detail, as well as the views of many contemporary observers of poverty who, over centuries, claimed the poor were often responsible for their own misery. Fecklessness, carelessness and drunkenness, they argued, were the real causes of poverty. Similar attitudes are evident even today. In a survey recently undertaken by the National Centre for Social Research 27 per cent of respondents, when asked 'why do you think there are families with children who live in need?', thought it was 'because of laziness or lack of willpower'. This compares with those who viewed poverty as 'an inevitable part of modern life' (31 per cent), due to 'an injustice in our society' (25 per cent) and those who considered the poor were poor 'because they have been unlucky' (10 per cent).[1]

The poverty endured by our ancestors was no more sharply defined than by the sight of thousands of homeless, orphaned and destitute children who eked out an existence by begging, crime or prostitution. In 1848 estimates suggest that in London alone 30,000 shelterless children were running wild. The extent of the problem warrants particular attention: Chapter 8 of this book explains how public and voluntary welfare organisations worked together to end the misery of underage vagrancy and abandonment.

Like that well-known sporting cliché, this book 'is a game of two halves'. The first two sections together examine the history of poverty from the medieval period through to the introduction of the modern welfare state. The third section, after a short introduction to family history, includes information on where records may be found to help trace and identify poor or pauper ancestors, a list of useful websites and a bibliography. Where topics benefit from further explanation, or where records are known to exist, these are explained in more detail in the appendices and highlighted in **bold** in the text.

There are, however, caveats in using the records section. It cannot, by definition, be an exhaustive list of resources and neither will it be entirely up to date. In recent years such has been the growth in genealogical studies that record and local study centres, family history societies and individuals are constantly adding to the stockpile of records, transcripts and files that are available to assist in the search for distant and not so distant ancestors, whether they were rich or poor.

Parts of this book have appeared before in various forms in *Ancestors* magazine, *Practical Family History, Family Tree Magazine* and *The Charter Town of Marazion* (1995).

Enjoy the experience of tracing your poor and pauper ancestors. But please don't get too despondent, upset or disillusioned if you find that a previously little-known relative turned out to be a vagrant down on his luck, or that a branch of the family had scraped together an existence, against intolerable odds, in a squalid urban tenement of eighteenth-century industrial Britain. It is after all, history now.

Robert Burlison
January 2009

ACKNOWLEDGEMENTS

Writing any history book – unless it is researched exclusively by an author in his own lifetime – invariably depends on the work of others. This book is no exception. I owe a debt of gratitude to the many writers and scholars past and present who have inspired, entertained and informed me while I researched and wrote this book. That said, errors and omissions are of course my own.

In writing this book I want to thank Simon Fowler, not only for his confidence in me to suggest the original idea, but also for his help along the way and with the illustrations. I would also like to thank Rupert Harding at Pen & Sword Books for his patience when at times other unrelated matters took precedence over writing. I am also grateful to Ray Whitehand of Historical Suffolk Research Service for his advice on the early Poor Laws and transcripts of documents. Last, but not least, a thank you must go to my wife, Lyn, for her encouragement and support. In particular for her secretarial skills and reading through what must have seemed like countless drafts and in keeping me supplied with endless cups of tea.

INTRODUCTION

Poverty has been a constant thread throughout history. At any one time a large mass of the population, possibly between one-third and one-half, struggled to survive on less than an adequate income, were badly housed – if housed at all – malnourished and forever susceptible to the ravages of sickness and disease. Poverty in theory could be guarded against by the more prudent – except that one of the causes of poverty was low wages which made financial planning against unemployment, sickness or death difficult, if not impossible.

The causes of poverty were various and often cumulative. When unemployment was (and still is) one of the major causes of poverty it followed disruptions caused by military conflict, the upheaval of land redistribution, the introduction of agricultural and industrial mechanisation and the effects of economic slumps. On a more intimate level, families were reduced to pauperism and dependent on state or private charity support as a result of inadequate or seasonal wages, sickness, old age or the death of the principal breadwinner. Yet it was only at the end of the nineteenth century that any serious attempts were made to understand the causes and nature of poverty. Seebolm Rowntree concluded from his studies in York – mirroring similar work undertaken by his contemporary Charles Booth in London – that poverty was primarily caused by low wages (52 per cent), the largeness of families (22 per cent), the death of the chief wage earner (15 per cent) and illness or old age (5 per cent).[1] Until then the view predominated that work was available to all who sought it and financial hardship was the result of an individual's moral failings, aggravated by unwarranted charitable support. Rowntree also argued that many, possibly most, members of the working class also descended into poverty at particular times of their life cycle: as young children, when they in turn had families or in old age.

It was a view reflected in a raft of almost entirely repressive legislation, first culminating in the Elizabethan Poor Law of 1601 and then repeated in the Poor Law (Amendment) Act of 1834. Vagrants, whether work seeking or work shy, were indiscriminately punished and parish officials were authorised to distribute poor-relief only to 'deserving' orphans, the sick and the aged poor. Apart from various state-aided initiatives, most of which had limited success, there was little positive help given to the genuine, work-seeking unemployed. The extent of poverty also gave impetus to a great outpouring of private charitable relief that at best kept the problem within reasonable bounds.

State-sponsored poor-relief, funded by the parish poor rate, was never intended on its own to support the deserving poor. From early Tudor times, government administrators looked to the private charity sector to produce most of the funds. And they did. Between 1480 and 1660 over £3 million was raised from charitable sources – a third of which was expended on the poor, either in outright relief or in areas of social rehabilitation. It was a theme that continued into the mid-nineteenth century and beyond. By 1862, over £1.6 million was raised in London alone for the impoverished poor compared to an estimated £1.4 million spent by the Metropolitan Poor Law authorities.[2]

There was considerable empathy and mutual support amongst poorer communities. In the eighteenth and nineteenth centuries the fear of poverty, together with the stigma associated with confinement in the workhouse, saw the creation of the friendly society movement which, like other self-help organisations, became a working class provider of assurance schemes to guard against unemployment or loss of work that resulted from sickness or old age. In rural districts and urban areas alike the poor shared food, organised childcare facilities and circulated out-grown clothing to those in their neighbourhood who were in a poorer, more impoverished state. They also cared for the sick and the elderly rather than see them consigned to the workhouse and found lodgings for the newly arrived and helped them search for work.

The Industrial Revolution, driven by the invention of the steam engine, powered Britain to global pre-eminence and earned it the title 'the workshop of the world'. It also created the world's first urbanised society. New towns grew around the mills, factories and foundries to house workers seduced by the prospect of high earnings and secure employment. This in turn created social problems on an unprecedented scale. The new industrial processes generated jobs but also had the ability to destroy them. Periodic trade depressions, characteristic of the new industrial economy, plunged thousands of workers at a time into unemployment. The Poor Law was not designed to deal with crises of this kind. By the end of the nineteenth century there was an increasing acknowledgement that unemployment was not the result of any failing on the part of an individual. This led in 1904 to the appointment of a Royal Commission to inquire into the suitability of the Poor Laws in industrial Britain. But when the Commission's findings were published the political and ideological landscape was beginning to change – demonstrated by the fact that the Commission could not agree on its recommendations and published 'majority' and 'minority' reports. A new Liberal government, encouraged by a landslide victory in 1906, was pursuing its own programme of social-welfare reforms to combat poverty in childhood, or as a result of low pay, unemployment, ill health and old age.

In 1908 the Children Act gave local authorities new powers to keep under-privileged children out of the workhouse. In 1909, old-age pensions, albeit with restrictions, were introduced and in the same year labour exchanges were set up to help the unemployed find work. Unemployment benefit began in 1911, as did health insurance for lower paid employees, although not initially for their families. These measures were evidence of a significant shift in public and political perception of poverty. This was exemplified in 1911 when the term 'able-bodied' disappeared from the Poor Law vocabulary and workhouses became 'institutions'.

The interregnum between the First and Second World Wars is marked by popular memories of unemployment. Fluctuations in the worldwide economy, exacerbated by the Wall Street crash in 1931, resulted in mass unemployment, prolonged periods of hardship and embittered social distress. The burdensome economic cost of unemployment – directly in benefit payments and indirectly through lost tax revenue – undermined the existence of the welfare measures introduced only twenty years earlier. In an effort to make and mend, benefits were cut, contributions increased and a means test introduced in an attempt to ensure the scheme remained viable.

In 1946 a newly elected Labour government introduced a National Insurance Act and, two years later, the National Heath Service Act. Far more comprehensive than its 1911 predecessor, the National Insurance Act, with its flat-rate contributions, insured everyone without exception against sickness, unemployment, industrial injury and old age. Its companion, the National Heath Service Act, created a universally free at point of use health service. There was a third piece of legislation enacted in those post-war years – one that was to mark the demise of the by then much-despised Poor Laws. With a preamble that included the dramatic words, 'the existing poor law shall cease to have effect', the National Assistance Act provided a less stigmatising safety net for the poor and the needy.

Absolute and relative poverty

There are two ways in which poverty can be defined. The first is absolute poverty where a person lacks the necessary food, clothing or shelter to survive. Absolute poverty is still widespread today in many developing countries, but rarer in modern industrialised societies where welfare benefits are available for the neediest. The second is to define poverty in a relative way based on the assumption that a certain standard of living is normal and those living below it, while not starving or homeless, are nevertheless poor.

Relative poverty was recognised in Tudor England when urban surveys were recording households containing 'persons who partly may live by labour and partly have the need of relief and comfort'. In the eighteenth century there were many people forced out of employment by land enclosure or the monumental changes in agriculture who were absolutely poor. There were others who were still thought of as poor even though they were able to gain access to the basic necessities of life.

In the late eighteenth century the pioneering economist Adam Smith defined absolute poverty as the absence of 'not only the commodities which are indispensably necessary for the support of life, but whatever the custom of the country renders it indecent for creditable people, even of the lowest order, to be without'. Throughout the period covered by this book there were, for example, 'rogues, vagabonds and vagrants' who were absolutely poor, but there were a far greater proportion who were relatively poor.

The deserving and the undeserving poor

Until the late nineteenth century many politicians, social commentators and providers of charitable support argued that the poor were responsible for their own misery. Carelessness, laziness and drunkenness, it was claimed, were the real causes of poverty. People who were poor as a result of these failings were considered as undeserving; they may have been given help, but it would be of the meanest kind. On the other hand, there was recognition that there were also those who lived honest, hardworking lives and were poor as a result of circumstances beyond their control. These were the deserving poor, the poor who had a greater moral claim to support in times of need.

As early as the twelfth century, monastic communities dispensing poor relief were wrestling with the problem of distinguishing between the deserving and the undeserving poor. Like their latter-day descendants, the greatest fear was in awarding too much support to the poor that would encourage immoral behaviour and reduce the incentive to lead responsible, independent lives. Caught between the worthy and the unworthy poor were the genuine, work-seeking unemployed. Many argued that if those were given support they would lose the incentive to work. Such a view led to a search for effective ways of providing sufficient help without encouraging pauperism (a pauper was someone in receipt of Poor Law payments) or dependence on the private charitable sector.

In the mid-eighteenth century the Poor Law authorities believed they had the answer. By subjecting the poor to the harshest of regimes it would, it was believed, encourage them to avoid becoming paupers altogether and enable them to lead independent lives. This principle was adopted in the eighteenth century when the 'workhouse test' was introduced and became enshrined in the 1834 Poor Law (Amendment) Act when the workhouse became central to the provision of poor relief.

Section 1

THE CAUSES OF POVERTY

Chapter 1

THE CAUSES OF POVERTY IN PRE-INDUSTRIAL BRITAIN

'For the poor always ye have with you'
John 12

In medieval times everyone, rich or poor, town artisan or country peasant, lived with the consequence of misfortune, when accidents, illness, disease or the premature death of a breadwinner had the ability to rob a family of its livelihood and home. Most of the population were vulnerable to deprivation at some stage in their lives but particularly at risk were the elderly and lone parents of young children. In this pre-industrial society the climate also determined living standards when economically good or bad years were measured against the quality of the harvest and its effect on grain prices. The unpredictability of the weather left people in a constant state of insecurity; in a bad year, spring frosts destroyed recently sown seeds or heavy summer rains ruined crops to create a scarcity of grain and high prices. Evidence of the 'calamity sensitive' nature of the period survives in the *Anglo-Saxon Chronicles*.. According to one monastic scribe in 1087,

> there was a very heavy and pestilent season in this land. Such a sickness came on man that full nigh every other man was in the worst disorder, that is, in the diarrhoea, and that so dreadfully, that many men died in the disorder. Afterwards came, through the badness of the weather as we before mentioned, so great a famine over all England, that many men died a miserable death through hunger.[1]

In the fourteenth century the 'Little Ice Age' produced a prolonged series of cold, wet summers resulting in a string of poor and mediocre harvests, dearth and famine. Torrential rain inundated and laid waste thousands of acres of farm land ruining some for years to come. Freshwater seas covered much of lowland Britain decimating cereal crops. The harvest of 1315 was the worst in living memory. Wheat that sold for 5s a quarter in 1313 was priced at 40s just two years later. A year's supply of barley, the cheapest grain, cost a family 60s and other foodstuffs rose comparably. Even when food was available, washed-away bridges and waterlogged roads prevented it from being transported. 'Six tenants are begging', wrote one resident of a Shropshire village, but before the autumn equinox, the six would become thousands. The poor suffered most from the dearth and devastation when 'they walked the fields, grazing like cattle; stood along roads begging; and searched behind alehouses and taverns for mouldy pieces of food'.[2] Others resorted to more extreme measures. According to the chronicler of the *Annals of Bermondsey*, the poor ate dogs, cats, the dung of doves and their own children to survive.[3] Corn discarded by harvesters traditionally became the property of the poor, but such was the shortage of food that even the wealthy were forced to glean from the fields. As the rains continued into 1316, and beyond, desperate crowds gathered in Canterbury to pray for 'a suitable serenity of the air', but to no avail. In the three-year period from 1315 an estimated 1/2 million people in Britain died from starvation, the ingestion of strange diets or the effect of putrid food as a consequence of crop failure and famine.[4] Devastating as it was, however, it was only a harbinger of things to come.

Bubonic plague, known to us as the Black Death, arrived in Britain during the summer of 1348, and by the time it had burned itself out eighteen months later, had killed almost one-third of the population creating an acute shortage of labour. In its aftermath fields were left unattended and those who had not died of the plague died of starvation. Plague was one factor in the demise of feudalism that brought about the free movement of labour and some protection against ruthless exploitation. Workers were able to command inflated rates from landowners short of labour. In 1349, at Yalding in Kent, Ralph, Earl of Stafford was forced to treble, from one penny a day, the wage paid to farm hands.

The breakdown of feudalism was a trigger in the creation of the earliest Poor Laws. To check inflation and improve the labour market the Ordinance of Labourers Act of 1349, together with the Statute of Labourers Act two years later, made it illegal to pay wages above pre-plague levels and to give alms to the able-bodied unemployed. At the same time arable land was increasingly turned to pasture when sheep rearing did not demand such a large labour force as crop growing and, in any event, there was less demand for crops. The plague had decimated rural settlements, but now landowners wanted the land on which the homes stood. Whole villages were destroyed and rural families were forced to flee. In the absence of alternative employment opportunities the problems of vagrancy began to assume ominous proportions.

In the fifteenth century poverty and vagrancy all too often went hand in hand. Virtually every corner of Britain had its quota of 'strong valiaunt beggars' existing on alms supplemented by begging and crime. Whether they were the genuine seeking work or the professional beggar, it became an established practice and children were brought up to know no other life. Many were merely a nuisance, but there were exceptions, particularly those displaced by military conflict.

The ending of the War of the Roses had produced from amongst the ranks of demobbed soldiers a class of itinerant beggars who – having been allowed to keep their arms to trade in lieu of pay – were armed. Further warfare saw even greater numbers of demobilised soldiers, and sailors, flood the labour market. In 1589, after an abortive incursion to Portugal, the Royal Navy landed its returning soldiers on the English coast only for a large number to find their way to London, where it took a squadron of dragoons to disperse the crowd intent on looting that year's Bartholomew Fair. The risk of civil disturbance increased when the landowning nobility turned from fractional strife to more peaceful means of estate management and in so doing discarded their quasi-military retainers. These redundant 'swashbuckling ruffians' were not easily absorbed into the local economy and added another dangerous element to a growing raggle-taggle band of wandering vagrants that comprised the dispossessed and the unemployed.

It was a situation not helped by a rising population. In the Elizabethan period, although national pandemics, such as an influenza outbreak in the 1550s, saw the population periodically fall, the overall increase may have been as high as 35 per cent.[5] This was not matched, however, by a corresponding increase in employment opportunities and in many parts of the country too many people were chasing too few jobs. There were major demographic changes too that influenced the availability of work when towns grew around specialised trades. Predominant amongst these and covering a wide geographical area was the cloth industry. This created prosperity for some but destitution for others after landowners sought more intensive, more efficient means of farming to meet the increasing urban demand for agricultural produce and in the process disposed of their surplus labour. Displaced from rural areas, where few alternative occupations existed, families were forced to take to the road in search of employment elsewhere. Enterprising solutions to feed a population that had grown as a result of longer life expectancy and increasing birth rates were not the only reasons tenant farmers lost their land: it was also driven by profit.

In meeting the demands of the cloth industry the production of wool provided a better financial return than arable farming. Landowners who grubbed out hedgerow and spinney turning small fields into larger, more profitable, less labour intensive sheep pasture were confidently assured they would see returns half as great again as derived from food production. But land enclosure proved to be one of the most controversial issues of the time. Stories surfaced of ruthless landowners, eager to maximise profits, evicting tenants from their homes and depopulating whole villages. By the time Sir Thomas More aired his concerns about a great social evil that caused much distress, the problems of land enclosure were sufficient enough to warrant investigation by a parliamentary commission. This led to an attempt to safeguard the employment of rural wage-earners when legislation ordered that every house with 20 acres or more should be 'adjudged a house of husbandry forever', and that those that had fallen into decay should be restored.[6] In the same year a further Act recognised that tillage was 'a principal means that people are set on to work and thereby withdrawn from idleness, drunkenness, unlawful gains and all other lewd practices', and ordered all grazing lands that had been arable for a period of twelve years prior to the start of Elizabeth's reign in 1558 should be restored to tillage and existing arable ground maintained in that condition.[7]

Whether the rural poor benefited from effectively freezing the agrarian economy in this way is debatable. According to one historian, the legislation was enacted, 'by men against whose own self interest its prescription ran, surely with full knowledge that it was unenforceable'.[8] The need for increasing food supplies and individual profit were further factors in the demise of the feudal system of land tenure. Families not only lost the land on which they had subsisted but also some degree of paternalistic and economic security that they, and generations before them, had once enjoyed.

The specialist trade (apart from agriculture) that employed more people than any other was the cloth industry. With a steadily increasing demand for textiles, it provided work for thousands of men, women and children throughout large areas of the country. Wool towns, as far apart as Totnes in Devon and Worstead in Norfolk, grew incredibly wealthy on the proceeds, and many families became wholly dependent on the trade for their livelihood. It was the first urban industrial complex of its kind, but it was also at the mercy of external events. Bad harvests, endemic diseases and military conflicts at home and abroad were liable to produce a downturn in the national economy, resulting in a fall off in demand and wholesale unemployment. The cloth industry was 'particularly subject to troughs of unemployment . . . and a breeder of poverty, even though it had come to be the employer of many thousands of people'.[9] And so it proved.

By the start of the seventeenth century the cloth industry was in recession. The government, sensing danger, attempted a rescue bid by compelling clothiers to assume a larger measure of social responsibility. 'Clothiers should [not] at their pleasure dismiss their work folk, who, being many in number and most of them of the poorer sort . . .' read a Privy Council Order circulated to affected areas in 1622. It also expected that wool merchants and clothiers 'who had profited greatly in good times, must now in the decay of trade . . . bear a part of the public losses as may best conduce to the good of the public and the maintenance of good trade'.[10] It was too little too late. By 1650, having lost its export market to overseas competition, the cloth trade fell into terminal decline. More crucially it precipitated the first industrial depression and spread unemployment from the industry to other involved artisan groups for which the country was ill prepared. Neither was the new breed of urban wage-earner prepared. In a situation that was to repeat itself during the 'second' Industrial Revolution of the mid-eighteenth century, those without work were more vulnerable than their rural cousins and more likely to resort to begging to survive. In the towns they were less able to engage in traditional pursuits to ward off starvation, benefit from the support of a paternalistic landowner or gain the empathy of a close-knit community.

Even when employment prospects were good, wage-earners were the victims of economic slumps that gave cause to rising inflation and a lowering in the standard of living. In the last years of his reign, Henry VIII ordered the debasement of coinage that resulted in the proportion of gold and silver in coinage being reduced. The effect was a reduction in the purchasing power of the wage-earner's income and the unskilled labourer suffered most. Their wage rates were already lagging behind prices but, without land-holdings or financial reserves, their meagre earnings proved insufficient to purchase the necessities of life. They had little alternative but to curb spending, seek the charity of others or starve. Amongst those who benefited from the devaluation of coinage were those engaged in the export trade, including the wool merchants and clothiers. Despite the vicissitudes of the industry, foreign merchants could now purchase cheaper English cloth. This in turn provided added stimuli to sheep rearing, a further spate of land enclosures and distress for even greater numbers of displaced smallholding farmers.

When Elizabeth ascended to the throne in 1558, her government replaced the debased coinage with a new issue, thus restoring currency to its correct level. But wage rates were further affected in 1563 by government moves to curb inflation. The Statute of Artificers was enacted to meet the shortage of agricultural workers resulting from the enclosure movement and the development of towns. All able-bodied men, women and children were ordered to work in the fields when required to do so. It also set upper wage levels for skilled workers and made it illegal to practise a craft without having first served a seven-year apprenticeship. But wage rates failed to keep pace with the rise in food prices and the standard of living continued to drop for many workers.

Until advancements were made in medical science, improvements to sanitation and better provision of public health, plagues and pestilence attacked the population, often on a cyclical basis, and left poverty and wholesale mortality in their wake. From the arrival of the Black Death in 1348, until it finally disappeared in 1666, the country was seldom free from this menace. Plague was random in its nature, sometimes affecting much of the kingdom, but at other times more selective. Norwich, for example, in a twenty-five-year period from 1579 experienced outbreaks every five years. It affected rural districts less than urban areas, where the poor, housed in crowded closely packed tenements, had little opportunity to escape contagion.

The death of a male breadwinner brought destitution to his family when, unless they were also afflicted, the earnings of his wife and children failed to compensate for the loss. For those who escaped infection a job might be lost if the employer had succumbed. The wealthier were able to flee contagious districts, but this resulted in an even greater loss to the poor when those who normally contributed to the poor rate disappeared. Furthermore, urban food supplies dried up when farmers were unprepared to risk infection by delivering produce to affected areas.

To forestall the event of food shortages in times of plague more enlightened authorities provided permanent corn stocks. The wisdom of this policy was clearly apparent at times of famine which, like plague, inflicted hardship on a regular basis. On average harvest failures occurred every four years, but more disastrous still, and a precursor to mass starvation, were periods of sequentially bad seasons. Particularly so were a succession of bad harvests in the 1590s that saw famine on a widespread scale. When food shortages led to increased prices it was the poor who inevitably suffered most. Perhaps one-fifth of the population in cities and one-tenth in rural districts lived on, or below, a subsistence wage.[11] The labouring classes were equally hard hit. Numbering between one-half to two-thirds of the population, the majority worked in agriculture. Here, subjected to the vagaries of the seasons and the climate, they enjoyed few guarantees of permanent employment and their meagre earnings needed to be stretched even further when food was in short supply and prices were high.

At times of dearth Acts of Parliament appeared regularly, dealing with most aspects of food supply, from price checking of bread and ale to restricting exports and preventing forestalling. Food riots became an often predictable response. In one case, poor cloth workers – having peacefully petitioned the authorities with their grievances over the price of grain and having not received an adequate response – boarded a ship in the Essex port of Maldon. They assaulted the crew, requisitioned grain and forced the ship to sea. The government, alarmed by its rebellious overtones, took firm action by arresting the alleged ringleaders and hanging four of them. Instances such as this, that were a direct response to the famines experienced in the last decade of the sixteenth century, provided an impetus for the Elizabethan Poor Law of 1601.

Chapter 2

THE CAUSES OF POVERTY IN THE INDUSTRIAL AGE

'everywhere I walked I met pale, lank, narrow-chested, hollowed eyed ghosts, cooped up in houses that were mere kennels to sleep and die in'
Frederick Engels, *The Condition of the Working Class in England*, 1844

Poverty was not, of course, unique to a time when Britain was ravaged by plague and predominantly a warring 'harvest-sensitive' agrarian nation. By the mid-eighteenth century the kingdom had entered a period of profound social and economic change when first water, then steam, replaced muscle and wind to power machinery for the mass production of manufactured goods. Rural craft skills and cottage industries were increasingly replaced by large-scale production in new 'manufactories'. Towns grew around the iron foundries, cotton mills and workshops of a new industrial Britain to house an influx of workers displaced from the countryside by inadequate sustainable wages or the titanic forces of land enclosure and mechanisation. The world's first industrial nation had created the world's first urbanised society. But this revolution in industry, together with its associated mass demographic movement of people, created social problems on an unprecedented scale.

Unhealthy, ill-ventilated and squalid crowded conditions greeted workers in the new 'manufactories', where machinery lacked little safeguard against injury or death. It was the era of factory rules and regulations when discipline was relentlessly and harshly meted out. It was where workers – more accustomed to nature's own time clock – found a life governed by the factory hooter and the rattle on the bedroom window as the knocker-up made his rounds. It was where employers eagerly took on women and young children to carry out dull, repetitive, debilitating tasks. It was where orphaned children were uprooted from the harsh confines of the workhouse to become pauper apprentices in the harsh confines of the workplace. And it was where in 1808 workers called for a wage increase, when adult male pay was 8s for an 84-hour working week.

Unhealthy, ill-ventilated and squalid crowded conditions also greeted workers in the houses they inhabited. In the mean streets that surrounded the factories of industrial Britain families lived cheek by jowl in ill-equipped terraces of back-to-back slums thrown up in a hurry to accommodate a soaring population. Moreover, inadequate, or non-existent, health provision and sanitation in these crowded tenements ('rookeries' as they were termed) saw chronic diseases such as cholera and dysentery spread unchecked causing the death of a breadwinner when all family members, but for the very youngest or the frailest of the elderly, were by necessity breadwinners. As the influx of workers grew – augmented by émigrés escaping the worst excesses of the mid-nineteenth-century Irish potato famine – families were forced to share homes and rent one room or a windowless, damp cellar.

Inclement weather and seasonal under-employment continued to inflict poverty on those engaged in agriculture. As too did inflation and economic slumps. But to the causes of poverty were now added the effects of industrialisation and urbanisation. The new industrial processes created jobs but also had the ability to destroy them. Periodic trade depressions, characteristic of the new industrial economy, plunged thousands of workers at a time into unemployment. What was once an isolated problem for an individual family, or a small rural community, became the collective problem of an enormous industrial working class concentrated in towns and cities across Britain.

One of the first to bring attention to the plight of the urban poor was factory owner and author Fredrick Engels. In his book, *The Condition of the Working Class in England* (1844), Engels included a social essay describing the slums of mid-nineteenth-century Manchester which, quoted at length, serves to illustrate the problems endured by those who lived with urban poverty.

> Here lie two groups of about two hundred cottages most of which are built on the back-to-back principle. Some four thousand people, mostly Irish, inhabit this slum. The cottages are very small, old and dirty, while streets are uneven, partly unpaved, not properly drained and full of ruts. Heaps of refuse, offal and sickening filth are everywhere interspersed with pools of stagnant

liquid. The atmosphere is polluted by the stench and is darkened by the thick smoke of a dozen factory chimneys. A horde of ragged women and children swarm about the streets and they are just as dirty as the pigs which wallow happily on the heaps of garbage and in the pools of filth . . . The inhabitants live in dilapidated cottages, the windows of which are broken and patched with oilskin. The creatures who inhabit these dwellings and even their dark, wet cellars, and who live confined amidst all this filth and foul air, must surly have sunk to the lowest level of humanity. That is the conclusion that must surely be drawn even by any visitor who examines the slum from the outside, without entering any of the dwellings. But his feelings of horror would be intensified if he were to discover that on average twenty people live in each of these little houses, which at the moment consist of two rooms, an attic and cellar. One privy – and that usually inaccessible – is shared by about one hundred and twenty people. In spite of all the warnings by doctors and in spite of alarm caused to the health authorities by the condition of Little Ireland during a cholera epidemic, the condition of this slum is practically the same in this year of grace 1844 as it was in 1831.[1]

Engels went on the report that 12 per cent of workers lived in cellars and estimated the total in Manchester to be 21,000. The common lodging house was also the focus of his attention which he concluded 'sleeps between twenty and thirty persons, in every room five or six beds are made up on the floor and human beings of both sexes are packed into them indiscriminately'.[2]

For those left behind to work in the fields, life was hard for the agricultural worker and his family. Rural family incomes, already depressed by periods of under-employment and seasonal work, were further eroded by inflation during the Napoleonic Wars that spanned the decades at the end of the eighteenth century. The spending power of wages continued to fall below prices during the war years until in 1820 the trend was reversed and the price of corn, for example, at 43s (£2.15) a quarter, became the lowest since 1793. It was a time of mixed fortune for those in agriculture. The high price of cereal crops and other foodstuffs brought prosperity to landowners and increased employment for labourers in the fields, but during a trade depression when food prices were low, although allowing for a marginally better standard of living, the effect was a lack of work. There were other

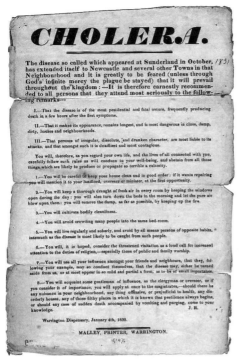

A cholera notice, 1832. In the overcrowded, unsanitary urban enclaves of industrial Britain disease was a frequent and unwelcome visitor. Notices, typical of the one seen here, were published with recommendations to avoid contagion. Although this notice acknowledges that damp and dirty houses are breeding grounds for the disease, it also suggests the avoidance of 'irregular, dissolute and drunken character[s]' as these, it considers, are at greatest risk of infection. (Reproduced by permission of Warrington Borough Council, Libraries, Heritage & Learning)

factors too that contributed to the worsening plight of the agricultural poor. The process of enclosing land deprived many of access to commons and wastes where free kindling was gathered, vegetables grown or pasturage available for a cow, a pig or for chickens to roam. The introduction of urban industrial processes also witnessed a decline in domestic rural handicrafts which once provided an essential supplementary income for those engaged in an industry so heavily dependent on the seasons or the climate. More labour-intensive methods of farming resulted from the introduction of first the seed drill and then the combine harvester. As a consequence, annual hirings began to give way to hirings of months or even weeks: in southern England at the start of the nineteenth century nearly one-half of all male hirings were for less than one year compared with 10 per cent only a generation before.[3]

Economic conditions were such in Ireland of the 1840s that a large section of the peasant-labouring classes, with tiny unviable plots of land, were reduced to pauperism. In unindustrialised Ireland, the vast majority of the native population depended on agriculture for survival, many of them on a single agriculture crop: the potato. The situation is described by the historian Robert Kee: 'He (The poorest peasant) lived off a tiny piece of land for which he paid such a high rent that almost all – and sometimes all – the cereal crops he grew on it had to be sold to pay the rent. He and his family subsisted on a plot of potato.'[4]

This class of peasant would be all too familiar with hunger for temporary periods during the 'slow' months of May, June and July when the old crop of potatoes was used up and the new crop not yet ready to eat. In addition to the poor economic conditions of the time, the 1840s saw the culmination of a vast population explosion in Ireland. Again, Robert Kee describes the effect, 'The pressure of this vast increase in numbers on the land became desperate, and land became subdivided into smaller and smaller plots on which more and more people subsisted mainly on potatoes. The poorest of all simply hired out their labour in return not for a wage, but for a small plot on which to grow them.'[5]

When the potato crop failed, $2^1/_2$ million of these labouring peasant classes became destitute, swelling the ranks of the Irish pauper classes and leading to the introduction of the Irish Poor Law Act of 1838 (see Chapter 5). During the famine years of the 1840s Ireland's workhouses became so overcrowded that the only way to deal with the excess was to encourage emigration. But so many clamoured to go – some even entering the workhouse for that sole purpose – that the option of emigration was restricted to those who had been workhouse inmates for at least two years.

Eventually, it was accepted that 'outdoor relief' should also be granted. This meant that paupers did not necessarily need to go into the workhouse but could nevertheless receive aid – including assistance to emigrate. Powers were granted to Boards of Guardians to enable them to contribute towards the cost of emigration, including providing clothing and paying the passage of any family that could prove it needed help. Between 1849 and 1906 nearly 45,000 emigrants were assisted in this manner.

In the years after the famine, government aid to Irish peasants was concentrated mainly on the western fringes of Ireland where there were high population levels coupled with low employment opportunities.

Apart from supplying the 'sinews of emigration' through assisted passages, the British government inadvertently encouraged others to assist aspiring emigrants. New taxes imposed for raising poor-relief encouraged landlords to limit their tax bill by reducing the number of poor peasants. Sometimes this could be achieved by 'forgiving' the rent, which would then be used to buy a passage, or by the landlord buying the tenant's home, land and crops at a price that would allow the family to emigrate.

While over 180 landlords and philanthropists offered some form of assistance to more than 80,000 emigrants – it was cheaper to pay for passages to Canada or America than to support the paupers at home – the bulk of assisted emigration was conducted by 10 major landlords who, between them, sent out some 30,000 people.[6]

In the British Isles, the combined effects of an agricultural depression, crop failure, changes to agricultural practises, together with a rising trend in the size of families, only served to exacerbate the problems of rural poverty. Increasingly workers, attracted by the prospect of more secure earnings and greater independence, started to move away to find employment in neighbouring industrial towns. And move they did. By 1851, for the first time, almost one-half of Britain's mainland population inhabited a town or city, and by 1901 three-quarters did so.

In the towns, although housing costs were higher and food needed to be brought, artisans and tradesmen generally enjoyed a better standard of living with wages, throughout much of the nineteenth century, that were twice that of the rural worker. Nevertheless, there were many extremely poor people in the towns who, like their counterparts in the country, were ill paid, badly housed and malnourished. But unlike the country districts, public health was a greater concern and a factor in a disparity between urban and rural mortality rates. According to the First Report of the Registrar General, published in 1839, in the agricultural districts of Yorkshire, Durham, Northumberland, Cumberland and Westmorland 204 out of every 1,000 inhabitants reached the age of 70 years, while in London it was 104, in Birmingham 81 and in Liverpool and Manchester 63.[7] It was a theme adopted by Edwin Chadwick when he turned his attention from amending the Poor Laws to an engagement with public-health matters (see Chapter 5). In his *Report on the Sanitary Condition of the Labouring Population of Great Britain* (1842), Chadwick provided graphic illustrations of living conditions amongst the lower urban classes and connected the prevalence of disease and high mortality to inadequate sanitary provisions, drainage and water supply. Although not acknowledged at the time, poor housing and inadequate diet also contributed to the spread of disease and put the poorest families at greatest risk. In the working class districts of major towns and cities, where population growth had made obsolete archaic sanitary facilities, the overall death rate during the 1840s increased from 21 to 31 per 1,000; with Birmingham doubling its rate to 27, and Liverpool rising from 21 to 34 per 1,000.[8]

Chadwick's work, together with the work of others, notably the Manchester physician James Kay, led in 1848 to the establishment of a national public-health authority, the General Board of Health, and a programme of public-health reforms that saw the provision of municipal sewerage systems, the supply of cleaner water and the demolition of unsanitary housing. But Chadwick and Kay were not alone in highlighting the plight and living conditions of the urban labouring classes in the nineteenth century.

Perturbed by the sight of what Frederick Engels described as 'pale, lank, narrow-chested, hollowed eyed ghosts, cooped up in houses that were mere kennels to sleep and die in', others were encouraged to venture an opinion on the plight of the urban poor. The journalist Henry Mayhew provided evidence of poverty in *London Labour and the London Poor* (1861) and Andrew Mearns, a Congregational minister, in his pamphlet *The Bitter Cry of Outcast London* (1883), wrote 'seething in the very centre of our great cities, concealed by the thinnest crust of civilisation and decency, is a vast mass of moral corruption, of heart-breaking misery, and absolute godlessness'.[9] When it was claimed as many as a quarter of London's inhabitants were living in poverty there were real fears it might lead to civil uprising. Amongst the nineteenth-century social commentators was Charles Booth, a partner in his family's prosperous steamship company, who, starting from the belief that the estimates were exaggerated, undertook a survey of poverty in London.

Booth's investigation – born out of an interest in arithmetical skills and a desire to apply more 'scientific' methods to the study of society – began with a pilot survey in Tower Hamlets in 1887, which was to last for fifteen years and was published in seventeen volumes as *Life and Labour of the People of London* between 1889 and 1903.[10] This massive survey was based on visits made to over 13,000 London streets between 1886 and 1891 with information obtained from a variety of sources: Poor Law relieving officers, school-board visitors, the police and house-to-house visitations. For the purposes of classification Booth divided the population into eight groups, ranging from Class H (the middle class and above) through to Class B (the casual poor) and Class A (the vagrant 'savage' and the criminal). Each was assessed as being either above or below a 'poverty line' which he set at a minimum income of between 18s and 21s a week for a family consisting of husband, wife and three children. Booth's work, much remembered for its street maps colour-coded according to social class and character, concluded that 30 per cent of the population of London were living in poverty, caused by low wages and industrial depression. Unlike many contemporary social commentators, Booth did not condemn the working classes for drinking, and saw it as a consequence of poverty as much as a cause of it. His estimates of Classes A and B were similar to those made by his namesake (but no relative) the Salvationist William Booth, who in 1890 calculated that one-tenth of the national population lived in desperate poverty. This 'submerged tenth', as he described them, comprised 'three million men, women and children [who were] a vast despairing multitude in a condition nominally free, but really enslaved'.[11] Charles Booth wrote critically of his lowest group, Class A: 'their life is the life of savages, with vicissitudes of extreme hardship and occasional excess. Their food is of the coarsest description, and their only luxury is drink. They render no useful service, they create no wealth; more often they destroy it. They degrade whatever they touch, and as individuals are perhaps incapable of improvement'.[12] Of his Class B, he was less critical but nevertheless considered them to be feckless, 'the lowest type of casuals, incapable of regular labour or of self-improvement'.[13] While Booth was tramping the streets of London and penning descriptions of the poorer classes, his work was being replicated by a member of a Quaker family whose business activity was the manufacture of chocolate.

Seebolm Rowntree, the son of Joseph – who, after identifying poverty, war, slavery, intemperance, opium and impunity as the 'great scourges of humanity', created the Joseph Rowntree Charitable Trust in 1904 – had been powerfully affected by a visit to the poorest parts of Newcastle and questioned whether Booth's findings would similarly apply outside London. In 1897, Rowntree commenced a study of poverty in his home town of York and published the results of his work in *Poverty: A Study of Town Life* (1901). This was a more refined study than that of Booth's, but nevertheless supported the findings of the London survey. It distinguished between 'primary poverty', where wages were insufficient to meet basic needs, and 'secondary poverty', when income was spent unwisely, either through extravagance or ignorance. Rowntree devised a food budget based on the rations set out by the Local Government Board recommended for those in the workhouse, and calculated the minimum necessary weekly expenditure for an adult was 5s 6d and 2s 10d for a child. He found that 9 per cent of the inhabitants of York were in primary poverty and 18 per cent in secondary poverty, a total of 27 per cent and very similar to Booths 30 per cent for London. Moreover, Rowntree analysed the causes of primary poverty and found that about half (52 per cent) resulted from low wages, and nearly a quarter (22 per cent) from the largeness of the family. Lower down the scale, the death of a breadwinner accounted for 16 per cent, illness of the principal breadwinner 5 per cent, irregular work 3 per cent and, reflecting the availability of low-paid work in York, unemployment 2 per cent. Rowntree also attempted to unravel the causes of poverty. In observing family circumstances he noted that the rewards of employment in normal times failed to meet the basic needs of life for many of the working population,

Seebolm Rowntree's Basic Adult Male Food Diet, 1899

The diet was the same from Wednesday to Saturday.

	Breakfast	Dinner	Supper
Sunday	Bread, 8oz Margarine, $^1/_2$oz Tea, 1 pint	Boiled Bacon, 3oz Pease Pudding, 12oz	Bread, 8oz Margarine, $^1/_2$oz Cocoa, 1 pint
Monday	Bread, 8oz Porridge, $1^1/_2$ pints	Potatoes with milk, 24oz Bread, 2oz Cheese, 2oz	Bread, 8oz Vegetable Broth, 1 pint Cheese, 2oz
Tuesday	Porridge, $1^1/_2$ pints Milk, 1 pint	Vegetable Broth, 1 pint Bread, 4oz Cheese, 2oz Dumplings, 8oz	Bread, 4oz Porridge, $1^1/_2$ pints

(From Howard Glennerster, John Hills, David Piachaud and Jo Webb, *One hundred years of poverty and policy* (Joseph Rowntree Foundation, 2004). Reproduced by permission of the Joseph Rowntree Foundation)

notably during childrearing, sickness, widowhood and old age. From this he later formulated his life cycle of poverty theory and published it in *The Human Needs of Nature* (1918).[14]

In 1913, when Rowntree turned his attention from the urban to the rural scene he found the plight of agricultural labourers was far worse than that of their urban cousins. Taking a weekly wage of £1 0s 6d as the minimum necessary to maintain a family of five on his 'poverty line', he found this was achieved in only five English counties – Derbyshire, Durham, Lancashire, Northumberland and Westmorland

The Life Cycle of Poverty

The life of a labourer is marked by five alternating periods of want and comparative plenty. During early childhood, unless the father is a skilled worker, he probably will be in poverty; this will last until he, or some of his brothers or sisters, begin to earn money and thus augment their father's wage sufficiently to raise the family above the poverty line. Then follows the period during which he is earning money and living under his parent's roof; for some portion of this period he will be earning more money than is required for lodging, food and clothes. This is his chance to save money. If he has saved enough to pay for furnishing a cottage, this period of comparative prosperity may continue after marriage until he has two or three children, when poverty will again overtake him. This period of poverty will last perhaps for ten years, i.e. until the first child is fourteen years old and begins to earn wages; but if there are any more than three children it may last longer. While the children are earning, and before they leave home to marry, the man enjoys another period of prosperity – possibly, however, only to sink back again into poverty when his children have married and left him, and he himself is too old to work, for his income has never permitted his saving enough for him and his wife to live upon for more than a very short time.

A labourer is thus in poverty, and therefore underfed –

(a) In childhood – when his constitution is being built up.

(b) In the early middle life – when he should be in his prime.

(c) In old age.

(From Howard Glennerster, John Hills, David Piachaud and Jo Webb, *One hundred years of poverty and policy* (Joseph Rowntree Foundation, 2004). Reproduced by permission of the Joseph Rowntree Foundation)

(Cumbria). Even allowing for areas where there was a higher family income, Rowntree was driven to conclude that 'the wage paid by farmers to agricultural labourers is, in the vast majority of cases, insufficient to maintain a family of average size in a state of mere physical efficiency'.[15]

Rowntree's work, as with Booth's, had its critics, most notably from the Charity Organisation Society. One of its members, Helen Bosanquet, who would later be appointed to a Royal Commission on the Poor Laws, argued nothing could be done for the lowest classes of the poor, except through the Poor Law (see Chapter 7). All that could be hoped was that with industrial progress they would gradually disappear. Despite the criticism, Rowntree's and Booth's work had a major impact on understanding poverty at the end of the nineteenth century. The similarity in their results suggested that poverty on this scale was a national rather than London problem. Rowntree's calculation of a primary poverty line added greatly to the debate on the causes of poverty. He was able to demonstrate that poverty was caused by circumstances, such as low wages or widowhood, which individuals had little control over. At a time when many believed poverty was caused by fecklessness or wasteful spending, Rowntree was able to evidence that 10 per cent of the population, however thrifty they were, had insufficient to live on. Moreover, his development of a poverty life cycle became influential in the formation of the early twentieth-century Liberal Party welfare policy when it aided the search for solutions to the problems of poverty.

Section 2

THE RESPONSES TO POVERTY

Chapter 3

EARLY STATE INTERVENTION

'for the necessary relief of the lame, impotent, old, blind and such
other among them, being poor, and not able to work . . .'
Preamble to the Act for the Relief of the Poor, 1601

At the end of the fifteenth century traditional forms of charitable
aid, notably from religious sources, were failing to keep pace
with the needs of a rising population. In times of acute
hardship the poor were increasingly forced to beg for survival and the
tendency to slip from pauper to vagrant became all too easy. There
were riots too that targeted those believed to be hoarding food in times
of scarcity or who put up prices unfairly. The problem of vagrancy,
with its inherent threat to civil unrest, worsened in 1485 when the War
of the Roses reached its climactic conclusion at Bosworth in
Leicestershire, releasing thousands of solders, penniless and unable to
find work, to roam the country as armed and desperate beggars.

In 1494, haunted by the spectre of insurrection, the government of the
newly enthroned Tudor monarch Henry VII introduced the first of a
series of Poor Laws to suppress begging and control the movement of
vagrants. When it was assumed the aged poor were taken care of by
religious or other charitable means, its purpose was to coerce and
punish the idle and dangerous poor. Like most of the Poor Laws that
succeeded it, no allowance was made for the unemployed and able-
bodied who genuinely wanted to work. In Tudor England, and indeed
until the nineteenth century, unless they were 'olde sick lame feble and
impotent persones not able to labour for their livyng',[1] the poor were
considered the victims of their own misfortune and it was assumed as
a matter of course that employment was available for all who sought it.

While condemning 'foolish pity and mercy' for vagrants, the
Vagabonds and Beggars Act of 1494 introduced a requirement that

beggars and other idle persons should be placed in the stocks for three days and fed bread and water before being whipped and returned to their place of origin. The Act was rarely enforced and it would take the effects of an economic depression in the opening decades of the next century to prompt the government into further action.

When diplomatic relations with the Low Countries were severed in the 1520s thousands of workers in the cloth industry were to find themselves without work. Concerns that this would lead to increased levels of vagrancy were heightened when it coincided with a run of bad harvests that created a dearth of foodstuffs. The government intervened by compelling clothiers to maintain existing levels of employment, and took action to control the price of cereal crops. An Act of 1531 was the first attempt to deal with the problem of the poor in so far as it distinguished between the impotent poor worthy of alms and the 'unworthy' idle beggar.[2] Vagrants were to be whipped before being returned to their place of birth or where they had dwelt previously for three years. Begging was permitted by the impotent poor, but only after being granted a licence to do so by magistrates. The unlicensed poor were to be fined, as were those who gave them alms. No provision was made for the able-bodied who genuinely sought work; forbidden to beg, they had little alterative but to break the law or face death by starvation.

The failure to address the needs of the able-bodied poor searching for work, which in itself drove up levels of vagrancy, would not be adequately dealt with until the next century. But in a draft of the next Poor Law – to make parishes legally responsible for their own impotent poor to curtail their wandering as beggars – there was at least the acknowledgement that insufficient work was available for the honest and able, work-seeking unemployed. The solution proposed by Tudor legislators – although it never reached the statute books – was for an elaborate scheme of public works on roads, harbours, bridges and ports. Notice was to be given of where jobs were available and all able-bodied unemployed would be expected to attend for work under threat of forced labour or conviction for felony. This was to be financed by a tax levied on parochial church collections and specially appointed parish officers would separate the old and infirm from those capable of work.

Because a proportion of parochial tithes were supposed to be reserved for the poor the parishes were expected to deal with their own problems of poverty. In 1536 an Act was passed requiring that 'all

Governors of Shires, Cities, Towns, Hundreds, Hamlets and Parishes shall find and keep every aged, poor and impotent person who was born or dwelt three years within the same limit by way of voluntary and charitable alms'.[3] In a further move to discourage begging, the offence of almsgiving was strengthened with fines of up to ten times the amount given. Children of the poor were to be taught a trade and, on reaching 11 years, set to work. The Act was at best partially successful but, like earlier legislation, it failed to distinguish between 'idle' able-bodied vagrants and those seeking work. According to one historian, 'Underlying the statute [of 1536] one still sees the stubbornly held persuasion that there were no genuine unemployed and vagrancy and beggary could be driven from the realm by the application of criminal law'.[4]

Behind all the Acts that were introduced in the sixteenth century lay the fear of insurrection. It was a concern that was particularly in the minds of Tudor legislators when 9-year-old Edward VI ascended to the throne in 1547. His lengthy minority inevitably introduced the possibility of power struggles and factional feuds and any increase in vagrancy would in such circumstances be dangerous. Fearful that they would become foot soldiers in an army of revolt, the government acted with almost unbridled savagery to rid the nation of the vagrant classes.

The most contentious clauses of a statute enacted in the first year of Edward's reign were reserved for vagrants and specified ferocious penalties. 'If any man or woman, able to work, should refuse to labour and live idly for three days, he or she should be branded with a red hot poker on the breast with the letter "V" and should be judged a slave for two years'.[5] Fed bread and water, with the occasional 'refuse of meat', slaves were expected to perform any task given them. If they refused then they were to be whipped, and imprisoned in leg irons. For recalcitrant offenders a lifetime of slavery or even death beckoned. In the event that nobody sought the services of a convicted vagrant it was ordered that he or she should be returned to their place of birth and there employed as a parish slave. There were even penalties for those who failed to mete out the punishment. Constables were threatened with two days in the stocks for neglecting to whip children or a fine of 5 marks for refusing to mutilate beggars.

The Act also required the enforced employment of vagrant children. They could be seized by anyone willing to teach them a trade, with boys apprenticed until they were 24 years and girls until 20. Seizure could take place without the parents' knowledge or consent and any attempt to reclaim their children could result in them being enslaved as well. The Act was not entirely oppressive. It prescribed weekly church collections for the impotent poor and invited parishes to erect houses for leprous and bedridden vagrants who could appoint persons to beg on their behalf by proxy. Despite these more humanitarian measures, even in these harsh Tudor times, the penalties for vagrancy proved a step too far and the legislation was repealed in 1550 and mandated a return to the provisions of earlier legislation.

In the mid-sixteenth century, as funds from religious sources were diminishing, hastened by the closure of the monasteries, parishioners were encouraged to provide funds for the impotent poor through weekly church collections. This was legislated for in an Act of 1551, which required parishes to register their poor and for the clergy to 'gently ask and demand of every man and women what they of their charity will be content to give weekly towards the relief of the lame, impotent and aged'.[6] In order 'to gather and collect the charitable alms of all the residue of people inhabiting the parish',[7] two collectors were appointed (a duty that often fell to the churchwardens to perform), and they also distributed the money collected to poor parishioners. The decision as to who should be awarded parish relief was left to the vestry – the governing body of the parish, who took its name from the room in the parish church where its members normally met. Although poor funds were usually collected at church services, bequests were also made by the more philanthropic members of the congregation. In Hackney, in what is now east London, for example, Thomas Heron, a painter by trade, bequeathed in his will that the rent collected from his cottage should be spent on the purchase of twelve penny loaves each Sunday for the poor.[8]

It was also in the mid-sixteenth century that the government took its first tentative steps towards the introduction of a compulsory rate for the relief of the poor. A decision made all the more easier in the knowledge that schemes were already operating successively at a local level in the provinces. Norwich had approved a compulsory poor rate, levied against all those with the ability to pay, in 1549. This was followed by similar arrangements in London, Lincoln and Cambridge, while the aldermen of York, having experimented with a poor rate in 1538 to relieve poverty experienced by plague victims, had made it a compulsory arrangement by 1550.

The principle was adopted nationally when church collections for the poor, encouraged by the Act of 1536, were made mandatory. Parish officials were authorised to report recalcitrant parishioners who declined to contribute to the poor box. Those who refused were summoned before a justice of the peace whose duty it was to fine the defaulter £10, assess their financial circumstances and order payment of a weekly sum under threat of imprisonment for non-compliance. Legislation also required the suppression of begging and parishes were empowered 'to appoint convenient places for the habitations and abidings of such classes' – an early reference to the provision of poor houses that later were to evolve into the **workhouse**.

Towards the end of the sixteenth century the collection of the poor rate was taken a stage further when – with similarities to its twenty-first-century council tax counterpart – legislation introduced a tax based on property. To meet the needs of the lawful poor, magistrates were empowered by an Act of 1572 to levy a household tax on all chargeable persons with the power to remand to gaol those who declined to pay the prescribed amount. Parishes were also required to complete a register of the impotent and aged poor, and to arrange for their relief, 'though always only in the home parish to which they were to repair and where they were to remain'.[9] All begging was prohibited, except in instances where the parish found itself unable to maintain a payment. In these instances, beggars were only to be licensed in their home parish. Those arriving from another parish were required to wear 'some notable badge or token, both on the breast and on the back of his outermost garment'.[10] The Act also introduced the office of overseer to the poor, to be appointed annually by a magistrate from 'substantial householders of the parish'. The duties of these unpaid officials, initially to assist churchwardens in their now greatly increased roles, steadily increased over the centuries until they had almost sole local responsibility for the poor.

The fear of the vagrant classes was clearly still paramount in the government's mind when the Act stipulated penalties far more severe than anything before; apart, that is, from the short-lived legislation of 1547. Vagrants were defined as 'all able bodied men without land or master who could not explain the source of their livelihood, [where] all such men who declined to accept employment, and by prescription certain classes of men, such as peddlers, tinkers and minstrels, who all too often proved to be vagrants'.[11] It totally outlawed the practice and miscreants were to be whipped and burned through the ear for the first offence; condemned as a slave for the second; and the death penalty for the third. In contrast to the Edwardian statue, there is evidence that the severe penalties were enforced. In the Middlesex **Quarter Sessions** between 1572 and 1575, for example, 44 vagrants were sentenced to be branded, 8 to be set in service and 5 to be hanged. Further evidence is available in recounting a period of eight months in the short life of one vagrant by the name of Joan Wynstone. 'She was first whipped and branded as a vagrant on 6 February 1576. The following July she was caught wandering again and only saved from hanging when her husband took her into service for two years. Still undeterred, she fled again at the first opportunity and was caught and sentenced to be hanged on 3 October'.[12]

The 1572 Act was the most substantive statute to date in the history of the early Poor Laws, but it failed to address the central problem of poverty: a lack of work for the genuinely unemployed. Without distinguishing between these or the 'idle' vagrant, an Act of 1576 ordered that stocks of raw materials, such as wool, hemp, flax and iron, were to be made available, at parish expense, on which the unemployed would be required to work.[13] In addition, houses of correction were to be erected to accommodate and reform 'incorrigible vagrants' who would be compelled to submit themselves to forced labour. Bastard children, who in the sixteenth century formed a large element of the vagrant classes, were given some degree of protection by the Act when it demanded that the mother and the known or reputed father were to be wholly responsible for the child's upbringing.

In the closing decade of the sixteenth century a series of disastrous harvests led to a severe economic depression. A succession of wet summers created a dearth of cereal crops that drove up food prices and rising levels of unemployment when fields became unworkable. There were also food riots and, even worse, death from starvation. Magistrates found it increasingly necessary to issue licences to beg and the possibility of famine saw bread riots in London and insurrection in the counties. In Oxfordshire, a group of twenty protestors were executed when they rebelled against the high price of corn, while in Somerset, where 'there was a considerable increase in the number of vagrants in these years' another forty persons were put to death upon conviction of felony.[14] Fearing spontaneous uprisings throughout the country, the government acted to prevent hoarding, prohibit the export of foodstuffs and to control prices. The clergy were instructed to encourage almsgiving and for parishioners to follow their example by observing two fast days each week.

Born out of necessity by the crisis the government enacted a series of statutes that dealt with the whole issue of poverty and vagrancy. The first, 'For the Punishment of Rogues, Vagabonds and Sturdy Beggars' in 1597, repealed earlier vagrancy laws and sought to deal severely and finally with the problem of rogues, vagabonds and sturdy beggars. It

Report by Overseers of the Poor

The Verdict of John Sprat & George Blome 'constable' Constables Edward Lombe & Willm Turner 'churchwarden' Churchwardens The sayd Edward Lomb John Deny & George Sawer 'overseers of the poor' Overseers of the pore taken the 19 day of July 1606.

To the first article we say that Thomas Turner & Symond Blome ar vittelers lycenced.

Tuching the setting of pore on worke the aged have as much works as they ar hable to do, but ther are dyverse pore mens children which myght be set to learn to spinne or knit wherein we desier yor worships Consent, vidz Nycholas Wodhouse, Ann Wodhouse, Marlye Metten, Robt Sallman, Thomas Sterby, Willm Johnson, Willm Graye, Margret Gray, John Fygge, Andrew Brinke

Tuching the bynding of Children to be apprentesses we have many vidz. Robt Metten, Peter Steward, Mathew Stewad, Willm Powle, Sammuell Powle Henry Porret, Willm Porret, Robert Tomsen, Willm Cooke, Willm Blome, John Lowes, Rychard Lowes & that George Sawer will with yor worships Consent take hym to be apprentice, Elizabeth Pettersen & that George Blome will lykewise take the sd Elizabeth & Temperance Wright [Losty will lykewise take ye sd] Ann Sterky, Ann [Sterky] Patterson Eddery Patterson Bullman Joan Whithed John Baldwin Joan Baldwin John Dennys least.

Tuching Roges ther hath passed on Margret Sheppherd which was sent from Haydon & was sent to Heverland & non other to or knowledges.

[Tuching other misdemenours] further we say that John Aldrege [ys] John Becke & Nycholas Wodhouse are common drinckers & the sd Wodhouse on the 7 day of this month had drinkin in his howse, one Gregory Johnson John Johnson kemers & John Becke & the sayd Wodhowse dyd then wilfully kyll a pygge of Symond Sallmons.

Extract from the report of the Overseers of the Poor for the Norfolk village of Cawston. Reports such as this provide an interesting account of rural life in early seventeenth-century England when it lists, amongst other things, 'pore mens children' set to work; the village's pauper apprentices; that one Margaret Sheppherd was removed (to another parish); and that John Becke and Nycholas Wodhouse 'did wilfully kyll a pygge'.

(Reproduced by permission of Norfolk Record Office (NRO, MC, 148/17-18))

required that anyone found begging was to be arrested, whipped 'until bloody' and returned to their birthplace or last residence. Upon arrival they were to be placed in service or, if judged incapable, lodged in an **almshouse**. Provision was also made for recidivists, who were to be banished from the realm or committed for their lifetime to a ship's galley.

Of far greater importance, and central to the issue of poverty, was the statute of 1598, entitled 'For the Relief of the Poor'. One of its principal aims was to extend the role of overseer of the poor. Although in existence since 1572, overseers were now empowered to set children to work when parents could not provide for them, as well as anybody else without any obvious means of maintaining themselves. All householders of sufficient means were to be taxed to provide for the purchase of materials on which the poor could be set to work and 'for the necessary relief of the lame, impotent, old, blind and such other being poor and not able to work'.[15]

Parish officials were also empowered to arrange apprenticeships for orphans and children of paupers from the age of 7, since this would relieve the parish of the cost of supporting the child. Apprenticeships were purportedly for children to learn a trade, but in effect provided a cheap supply of labour for those who needed agricultural or domestic servants and factory workers. Suitable dwellings for the poor, financed from the poor rate, were also to be provided, usually in the form of an almshouse. Overseers were required to keep parish records and provide magistrates with an annual account of their activities and finances. Failure to do so, or if they were in any way negligent, resulted in these unpaid officials being liable to incur a hefty fine of 20s (equivalent to about £100 today). If insufficient taxes were raised within individual parishes, magistrates were able to spread the rate across other parishes within the county. They also had the power to seize the goods of recalcitrant taxpayers or to commit them to prison until the debt was paid.

The surviving accounts of the overseer in the Cornish parish of Marazion provide an example of the expenditure to the needy, which took the form of either weekly relief or an occasional handout as necessity demanded. This might take the form of money, food, fuel or clothing. Medical treatment and funeral expenses were also provided. 'Ould Grace Garland' appears each year in the accounts from 1650 until 1663, when 3s 4d was spent on a shroud for her, 1s 2d paid for 'bread, beere and candalls, sending for the Prist [priest] and washing

Accounts of the Churchwardens and Overseers of Great Melton, Norfolk

The account of John Browne and Edward Bunne Churchwardens and overseers of the poore of the towne and p[ar]ish of great Melton for the yeare 1648 made and give[n] up march 29 1649

Impri[im]is Recd by the accomptants of Thomas Sherwood Churchwarden & Ao 1647 as arreares in his hands upo[n] his accompt	1 - 5 - 1
It received of Tho: Weston Churchwarden p[ar] Ao 1646 p[ar]t of the arreares in his hands	1 - 10 - 0
It recd for 12 moneths Collecc[i]on at 9s ob qr p[ar] mens[i]s	5 - 8 - 9
Sum[m]a tot recd	8 - 3 - 10
Out of w[hi]ch disbursed To the widowe Johnson for 51 weekes Collecc[i]on at 4d p[er] weeke	0 - 17 - 0
To the widdow Richardson for 51 weeks at 10d p[er] weeke	2 - 2 - 6
To James Brand for 12 weeks at 12d p[er] week	0 - 12 - 0
ffor housrent for the widd Johnson for half a yeare ended at Michs 1648	0 - 6 - 0
ffor fewell bought for the wid Richardso[n] w[i]th 12d for the carringe	0 - 4 - 0
To Roger Baxter at 3 sev[er]all tymes for himselfe and the vid Baly	0 - 7 - 6
Paid to make up the summe of 4li for Robt Goodreds diet & cloathing for one whole yeare ended at Hollomas last 1648	0 - 14 - 6
Given to poore passengers	0 - 0 - 6
Laid out for the warrant for overseers	0 - 0 - 4
ffor making the rates & there accounts and entering them into the Towne booke	0 - 1 - 6

deduct for o[u]r expenses in passing
this account & collecting the money   0 - 1 - 6
Sum[m]a tot. disbursed   5 - 8 - 10

So there remaynes in these accomptants hands w [hi] ch they are ready to pay over to ye
succeeding officers the summe of   2 - 15 - 0

Townestocke
In the hands of Edm. Burton   10li
In the hands of Edw. Parke junior   9li
In the hands of Tho: Parke w[hi]ch
was money that Tho: Weston had   10li
In the hands of Mr Edm Anguish
In the hands of Mr Edm. Anguish of old   10li
It more in his hands of the money recd of John Baly   3li
It more in his hand yt was Baxters guift   5li
In John Balyes hands ye remaynder of 10li
and upo[n] his bond (besides 6d. charges)   2li
                                                                       41li

The monthly Taxac[i]on p [ar] Ao 1648 John Browne & Edw: Bunne Ch.wardens Apr. 3.
1648
Edm: Anguish gent   0 - 8
Geo: Bayfield gent   0 - 10 - ob
Thomas Sherwood   0 - 6
Joh. Banks senr   0 - 10 - ob
Anne Rawlyn vid   0 - 5
Thomas Parke   0 - 5 - ob
Ffranc. Wale & John Baly   0 - 3
Edward Rowland   0 - 3
Thomas Rob[er]ts   0 - 2
Tho:Weston   0 - 2 - ob
John Browne   0 - 1 - ob qr
Tho: Ffox jnr   0 - 2 - ob
Robt Spencer   0 - 2 - ob
Mich. Smith   0 - 2 - ob
Will Read & Wm. Dey   0 - 2 - qr
Martin Bucke   0 - 1 - qr
Ffrances Smith   0 - 1 - qr
Willm Ffranklin   0 - 1 - ob
Edm. Bishopp   0 - 0 - ob qr
Nich. Lightwin   0 - 0 - ob
Willm Juby   0 - 0 - ob
Thomas Ffunnell   0 - 1

Ephr. Jackler	0 - 0 - ob qr
Joh. Bankes junr	0 - 0 - ob qr
xxofer Nobbs	0 - 0 - ob
John Heigooday	0 - 1 - qr
Richard Davy	0 - 1 - qr
Edward Bunne	0 - 1 - qr
John Bale	0 - 0 - ob
Robt Parke	0 - 0 - ob
Robt Gobart Clerke	0 - 5
Willm Younger Clerke	0 - 5
Mrs. Jermy	0 - 5
Henry Capps gent	0 - 6 - ob
John Smith of Hetherset	0 - 3
Sr John Palgrave knight	0 - 1 - qr
Wid Rackh[a]m	0 - 0 - ob
Steven Colman	0 - 0 - ob
Willm Younger Cl. for the? Cities? lands	9s 0d 3/4
	p[er] mens[i]s

Edmond. Anguish
Geo: Bayfield
W Yonger

(Reproduced by permission of Norfolk Record Office (NRO, EVL645, 463X9, 1631–1694))

and shrouding her', 6d 'at her buring' and 6d 'to the bedesman [the sexton]'. Like other coastal parishes, the dangers of the sea are also evident in Marazion's accounts; payments 'to the seaman' are common as are the entries that poignantly record 'making the grave for the seaman'.[16]

The Act of 1598 also intended that parishes were finally to rid themselves of the problem of vagrancy and ordered that 'no person shall go wandering aboard and beg in any place whatsoever, by licence or without, upon pain to be taken and punished as a rogue'. It acknowledged that insufficient funds may be collected by the poor rate alone and allowed begging in certain situations 'save only for poor inhabitants of a parish who might, upon determination of the overseer, be permitted within their own parish to ask relief of victuals'.[17]

The Act, setting out procedures to deal with all categories of the poor, the impotent, the unemployed and the vagrant was a watershed in the history of the Poor Laws. It remained in force – save for its

ABSTRACT OF THE PARISH ACCOUNTS,

FROM THE 15th MARCH, 1834, TO THE 13th SEPTEMBER, 1834, (BEING TWENTY-SIX WEEKS.)

Mr WILLIAM BAKER, Penton, — WILLIAM PARKER, Shelton, } *Churchwardens.*

Mr THOMAS HINDLE, Stoke, — JOHN GOODWIN, Lane-End, — GEORGE JAMES, Hanley, — WILLIAM WEAR, Shelton, } *Overseers.*

Receipts			£ s. D	£ s. D	Disbursements.	£ s. D	£ s. D	£ s. D
To Cash, Third Rate, 1832—3,	Small		2 3 4		By Bal. due to the Overseers from the last half yearly statement, March 15			120 1 6½
— Fourth		Large	0 17 11	2 3 4	Clothing and Bedding for the Workhouse	56 1 11		
— Fifth		Do	0 7 6	0 17 11	Provisions for the Workhouse	88 6 6½		
				0 7 6	Miscellanies for the Workhouse	50 6 4½		
— First 1833—4,		Do	24 11 9		Building and Repairs	47 0 2		
— First		Small	13 8 6		Assessed Taxes	2 11 11½		
				38 0 3	Bread Baker £15 10s, Barber £4 14s 6d	20 4 6		
— Second		Large	87 10 6½		Schoolmaster £9 18s, Schoolmistress £6 10s	16 8 0		
— Second		Small	100 15 9½		Porter £4 6s, Watchman 13s	4 19 0		
				249 6 4	Rent of the Workhouse	72 2 3		
— Third		Large	350 3 5½		Governor, on account	7 19 5		366 0 1¼
— Third		Small	330 11 8½					
				680 15 2	Bastardy Payments	413 2 10		
— Fourth		Large	997 9 6		Collector's Salary	24 5 5		437 8 3
— Fourth		Small	321 14 8½					
				1319 4 2½	Pensioners	706 16 10½		
— First 1834—5,		Large & Small	2272 1 6		Poor belonging other Parishes	98 1 0		804 17 10½
				2272 1 6	Weekly payments to Out Poor, Incidental	1854 12 11½		
— Second		Do	901 8 8½		— Permanent	1089 14 0		
				901 8 8½				2804 7 8½
				5463 4 11	Surgeons			45 2 9
					County Rates			319 17 6
Sale of Marbles made in the Workhouse			2 5 9		Lunatic Asylum £100, Constables' Accounts £26 7s 0d			126 7 9
Paupers' Earnings out of the house			56 0 0		Justices' Clerks' fees			31 4 0
From Fathers of Illegitimate Children			326 6 4		Assistant Overseers' Expenses at Justices' Meetings			10 7 10
From other Parishes for their Poor			59 0 11		Expenses in proving settlements			3 16 7
From Collector of Excise for Pensioners			694 4 2½		Incidental payments			79 10 5
From County Voters			1 17 0		Expenses removing of Paupers to their own Parishes			8 1 10½
Incidental Receipts			43 19 2		Coffins and funeral fees			64 4 2
				1183 13 10½	Tolls and postages £8 2s 3½d, Horse hire £2 12s 6d			10 14 9½
				6646 18 9½	Rent, Repairs, &c., of Parish Office			3 16 6
					Wheelbarrows, Planks, &c.			10 4 9
					Expenses keeping Parish Horse, Ass, Carts, &c			0 7 6
					Printing, Stationery, and Advertisements			3 17 0
					Appeals £17 9s 11d, Apprentice fees £10			27 9 11
					Suspended orders			6 16 4
					Solicitor £7 16s, Auditor £5 8s			13 4 0
					County Voters			1 0 0
					Assistant Overseers' Salaries			220 12 11
Balance due to the Overseers				45 3 1	Collectors' Salaries			144 3 9½
					Superintendent of Pauper Labourers			20 16 0
					Old debts £901 6s 0d, Loan money repaid £20			921 6 0
				£6692 1 10½				£6692 1 10½

Parish accounts. Churchwardens and Overseers of the Poor were required to produce regular accounts of all poor-relief receipts and disbursements. In this example the accounts prepared for the Staffordshire parish of Penkhull show that £5,463 4s 11d was collected from the parish rate with other sources of income including the proceeds from the sale of marble produced by workhouse inmates and receipts from fathers charged with the responsibility for their illegitimate children. On the payments side, in addition to providing for the workhouse, other major items of expenditure were bastardy payments and pensions. It also includes the sum of £98 1s for the 'Poor belonging to another parish' which might suggest these were the newly arrived, awaiting the issue of a settlement certificate or their removal back to the parish of their birth. (Reproduced by permission of Richard Talbot, Stoke-on-Trent College)

largely unchanged re-enactment in 1601 by a same named 'For the Relief of the Poor' Act (often referred to as the 43rd Elizabeth) – for almost 250 years. It made each parish an administrative unit and responsible for its own poor-relief because it was there that individual circumstances were best known. This was also based on the assumption that a stable, non-migratory society offered fewer social perils. This assumption, which in practice severely restricted the movement of labour, would be tested in the eighteenth century when, as the Industrial Revolution gathered pace, many thousands of migratory workers left rural areas to seek their fortune in the new industrial towns.

Following the '43rd Elizabeth' one of the last and undoubtedly the most unpopular and contentious of early Poor Laws was the Act 'For the better Relief of the Poor of this Kingdom', commonly referred to as the 'Act of Settlement'. Introduced in 1662 – under pressure from parishes needing stronger powers to rid themselves of unwanted migrants – it empowered magistrates to examine, remove and return to their original parish any newcomers who were 'likely to be chargeable' to the parish poor rate. Since the fourteenth century, when a proportion of parochial tithes was supposed to be reserved for the poor, the notion that everyone had a parish to return to if found wandering was implicit in much of the early legislation. This was now legislated for and only allowed migrants to settle in their adopted parish subject to having lived there unchallenged for forty days. Should a complaint be made to the overseer, migrants would be ordered back to their last place of settlement, unless they could prove that, by renting a property worth £10 or more a year, they were unlikely to claim poor-relief. When the average labourer's cottage was valued at no more than £5 a year, only the more comfortably off were certain of being safe from being issued with a **removal order**. In practice almost everyone, whether the idle beggar or the industrious and law-abiding, risked being returned to the parish they had wanted to escape from. Even harsher conditions followed. In 1692, in addition to paying rent to a prescribed level, migrants were only entitled to remain in their chosen parish by subscribing to the poor rate or being hired for work for at least one year. This was the principal reason for annual hiring fairs to be held on the same day each year to ensure workers were only engaged for 364 days at a time. Women gained a settlement by marriage, but a child's place of settlement – until they reached the age of 7 when they were old enough to be bound by an apprenticeship – was that of the father's.

In 1697 an Act was introduced that allowed overseers to grant **settlement certificates** to those who sought work in another parish.[18] If the 'certificate man' then subsequently fell on hard times in his new parish (or was seen as a potential candidate for poor-relief) the original parish was obliged to accept him back and award relief to him and his

Transcript of a Vagrant's Pass

Norff Wheras the bearer hereof Thomas Joanes of St. Mary Martin in London was then vagrant in oure parish of Tasbergh in the county of Norffolke & hath received correction according to lawe in that case p[ro]vided These are in his Ma[jes]ties name to charge & require all you whom it may concerne to conveigh or cause to be conveighed the sayd Thomas from constable to constable ontill he shall come to the place aforesayd hereof fayle not as you will answer the Contrary & further we desyre you to give him releife & loging as may be convenient Tasbergh December 15 1630

(Reproduced by permission of Norfolk Record Office (NRO, MC, 54/33))

family. In this event, recipients were required to wear a badge featuring a capital 'P' on their clothing to denote their entitlement to parish relief – a practice that was destined to survive until the nineteenth century.

Poor families, subjected to the laws of settlement, spent much of their lives moving around the country. In February 1748 Edward Melling, a tailor, also an inmate of the Marazion workhouse with his wife Elizabeth and five children, was examined by magistrates and said that he had been born on Tresco, 'one of the Islands of Scilly'. He had been bound as an apprentice to John Hitchens of Penzance, where he stayed for nearly three years, but his master 'failing and going off' he moved to London 'and several other places', until 'a couple of years ago he set up in business in Marazion; he married his present wife in [nearby] Lelant eighteen years ago'.[19]

Also in Cornwall, a much sadder tale is told of Mary Saunders. Mary was examined by magistrates in July 1766 with her children, Mary, aged 16, Anne, aged 12, Elizabeth, aged 5, Ursula, aged 3, and Christian, aged 9 months. According to surviving settlement papers she had been born in Perranuthnoe and at 14 went to work as a servant with William Laity of Marazion. Three years later she went to Penryn to work for a Mr Hawke and then moved to Plymouth where she married William Saunders, a mariner. For the next ten years she lived 'at different places in Devon, shifting her habitation just as the service which her husband was employed in required'. In 1753 the family moved to Marazion, where William worked 'partly in the fishery, partly going to foreign parts in the merchant service and during the six years of the late war was in His Majesty's service on board different

An Eighteenth-century Settlement Examination

The examination of William King now of the parish of St Clements Ipswich aforesaid mariner taken this 29 Jan 1776.

Who on his oath saith that as he has now been informed he was born in the parish of St Clements Ipswich where his father John King resided by virtue of a certificate granted by the parish of Woodbridge in the said county in the year 1703. acknowledging Robert King (father of the sd John) and his wife to be settled inhabitants in the sd parish of Woodbridge and this examinant saith that about 8 years agone (sic) he was rated to and paid the poor rates in the said parish of St Clements and that the examinant hath done no art to gain a settlement otherwise than above

the mark of Wm King

Sworn before us

W Clarke

Joseph Clarke

(Transcript reproduced by permission of Historical Suffolk Research Service (Source: Suffolk Record Office Ref: FB98/G1/31))

ships of war'. Her husband left home 'about eleven weeks since, but where he is gone she knows not, nor ever heard, but he said that he was born in Llanrhian in Pembroke in south Wales, and that his place of settlement was there'. Mary was unable to prove her own original place of settlement by work and, as a wife took her husband's place of settlement, was removed to south Wales.[20]

At the end of the eighteenth century further legislation ensured that no one was removed from a parish until they actually became a charge on the poor rate; apart that is from pregnant, unmarried women who were potentially the most expensive drain on the poor rate. It was not unknown for an impoverished woman in the advanced stages of pregnancy to be unceremoniously removed by the overseer beyond the parish boundary to ensure the child would be another parish's financial burden. Although amendments were made to the settlement laws, notably in 1846, when there was a right to settlement after five years' residency, and in 1865, when all settlement powers were placed in the hands of Boards of Guardians, the law of settlement was not finally abolished until 1948.

The exclusive nature of settlement did have some benefits. Paupers in their home parish engendered sympathy from their neighbours and from the overseer of the poor, who ensured they did not actually starve and made life as comfortable as could be expected for those who had genuinely fallen on hard times. However, enactment of the laws of settlement became a bureaucratic nightmare as magistrates heard appeal after appeal against removals and arbitrated in disputes with neighbouring parishes. 'Very difficult to be executed, vexatious to the poor and of little advantage to the public' was how they were condemned in a 1735 parliamentary report. The policy of removing migrants, often within two adjacent parishes, or when individual family members had different places of settlement, invoked considerable legal argument and proved to be a powerful case for the later establishment of **Poor Law unions**.

Provision for illegitimate children was made in a series of **bastardy** acts introduced between 1732 and 1744. Until 1732, it was sufficient only for an unmarried woman to declare her pregnancy to the overseer and name the father. This was then extended to require the father to maintain his child, but failure to do so would incur a custodial sentence. With the father in prison, the parish provided poor-relief to the mother and child until the father was able to secure his release. This he did by agreeing to support his family and reimburse the relief paid during his period of incarceration. Under the terms of a statute passed in 1744, illegitimate children were granted the same settlement as the mother, regardless of where they were born.[21] For fathers who abandoned their wives and family to the support of the parish and 'lived idly, refused work or begged', punishment of up to one month in a 'house of correction' was also prescribed.

In 1723 an Act, more commonly referred to by the name of its sponsor as the (Sir Edward) Knatchbull Act, entitled parishes singly, or jointly with neighbouring parishes, to establish a workhouse for the 'keeping and employing of poor persons; and there they are to keep them, and take the benefit of their work and labour, for the better maintenance and relief of such persons'. For those who refused to enter a workhouse, 'they were to be put off the parish books' and forfeit any entitlement to poor-relief.[22]

The first person credited with operating a workhouse as a deterrent was Matthew Marryot, who argued that 'the advantage of the workhouse to the parish does not arise from what the poor people can do towards their own subsistence, but from the apprehension that the poor have of it'.[23] It was Marryot's success at the start of the eighteenth century in promoting a number of establishments in southern England that encouraged the government to continue his idea. Within a few years of the introduction of the Knatchbull Act 150 workhouses had been opened, with parishes reporting a saving in poor-relief payments. Bradford, in Wiltshire, for example, provided a workhouse in 1727 and claimed by 1731 to have reduced its annual poor relief from £800 to £400. In ensuring the workhouse acted as a deterrent to the able-bodied, only the desperate, it was argued, would accept the strict regime of forced labour in return for accommodation. That this was achieved is evidenced by one resident in the Yorkshire town of Beverley:

> on opening the workhouse notice was given to the poor that the weekly pension [poor relief] was to cease and that such as were not able to maintain themselves . . . might apply to the governors of the workhouse. The result of this was that though before opening of the house 116 persons received the parish allowance, not above eight came in at first and in the subsequent winter the number in the house never exceeded twenty-six, although all kinds of provisions were very dear and the season was sickly.[24]

Costs however, in setting up and operating a workhouse often exceeded slender parish resources and schemes were introduced to do this jointly with adjacent parishes.

As early as 1696 a local Act incorporated eighteen parishes in Bristol for the purposes of jointly establishing a workhouse to accommodate and train pauper children. This was followed by similar civic incorporations in, for example, Exeter, Gloucester, Worcester and Plymouth. These towns administered their own poor relief with workhouses (or alternatively houses of industry) where the poor could be taught useful skills and at the same time earn their keep, thus sparing the ratepayers the responsibility of providing for them. By the mid-eighteenth century, encouraged by savings reportedly made to the poor rate, the idea soon spread. In Suffolk, for example, the parishes of St James' and St Mary's were incorporated for the purposes of erecting a workhouse 'for the better employing and maintaining the poor within the Burgh of Bury Saint Edmonds'.[25] In 1748, the Incorporation – managed by 'twelve persons chosen out of the honestest and discreetest inhabitants [of the town] occupying tenements of 8s yearly rent'[26] – paid one Thomas Woodroffe the sum of £420 for a property and converted it into a workhouse large enough to accommodate 250 inmates. By 1776, the year in which the first official workhouse returns were made, almost 2,000 were in operation at parish level in England and Wales – representing approximately 1 for every 7 parishes.

The practice of organising poor relief on a local collective basis was endorsed at national level. In 1782 the Act 'For the Better Relief and Employment of the Poor' aimed to organise poor relief within a large group of parishes. Workhouses in these 'unions' were to be provided for the sick, the aged and the orphaned poor. Significantly, able-bodied paupers were not to be admitted, but were to receive outdoor relief or found work in their home parish, with employers reimbursed from the poor rate for the additional labour costs. The Act, known by the name of its sponsoring Member of Parliament Sir Thomas Gilbert, also sought to improve the administration of poor relief with the appointment of Boards of Guardians. These management committees, comprising representatives from participating parishes, were appointed by magistrates and charged with the responsibility of finding work for the 'able bodied and otherwise to cause such person or persons to be properly maintained, lodged and provided for, until such employment shall be procured'.[27] The measures outlined in the Gilbert Act were adoptive only, but when it endorsed the controversial practice of outdoor relief – something that remained an anathema to the many who held the belief that the able-bodied were idle only by choice – less than seventy 'Gilbert Unions' were established.

At the end of the eighteenth century, with Britain engaged in the Napoleonic Wars, the import of foodstuffs became scarce. This, combined with a series of bad harvests at home, created high bread prices and food shortages. To avert the possibility of civil disturbance parishes attempted to supplement the earnings of the less well paid with an allowance related the prevailing price of bread. Payments differed from parish to parish but its principles were derived from a scheme introduced in the Berkshire village of Speenhamland. Here, magistrates, concerned at the level of food shortage and deprivation, introduced an allowance to enable labourers to have their income supplemented to subsistence level by the parish, according to the price of bread and the number of children in the family. Until labour rates began to be determined by the Employment of Labourers Act in 1832, the 'Speenhamland System', as it became known, was widely

Notice of Speenlandham System

That it is not expedient for the Magistrates to grant that assistance by regulating the Wages of Day Labourers, according to the directions of the Statutes of the 5th Elizabeth and 1st James: But the Magistrates very earnestly recommend to the Farmers and others throughout the county, to increase the pay of their Labourers in proportion to the present price of provisions; and agreeable thereto, the Magistrates now present, have unanimously resolved that they will, in their present divisions, make the following calculations and allowances for relief of all poor and industrious men and their families, who to the satisfaction of the justices of their Parishes, shall endeavour (as far as they can) for their own support and maintenance.

That is to say, when a Gallon Loaf of Second Flour, weighting 8lb.11ozs shall cost 1s then every poor and industrious man shall have for his own support 3s weekly, either produced by his own or family's labour, or an allowance from the poor rates, and for the support of his wife and every other of his family, 1s 6d. When a Gallon Loaf shall cost 1s.4d, then every poor and industrious man shall have 4s weekly for his own and 1s, and 10d for the support of every other of his family. And so in proportion, as the price of bread rise or falls (that is to say) 3d to the man, and 1d to every other of his family, on every 1d which the loaf rise above 1s.

By order of the Meeting

W. Budd, Deputy Clerk of the Peace.

(Minutes of a meeting, dated 6 May 1795, at the Pelican Inn in Speenhamland, Berkshire, when magistrates first authorised the payment of supplementary poor relief, based on the price of bread).

adopted by parishes in southern England and is thought to have saved many families from starvation.

Early Poor Laws in Scotland followed a different path. Legislation in 1424 distinguished between the able-bodied poor and those who, due to age, infirmity or sickness, were obliged to resort to seeking charity aid.[28] Begging was permitted, but those under 14 years of age or over 70 years were not allowed to do so, unless unable to work. The able-bodied poor found begging risked being arrested and only released from incarceration for a forty-day period to enable them to find work.

In 1535 an Act 'For the Stanching of Maisterfull Beggaris'[29] established that the poor were only to beg in their home parish and in 1579 a further statute categorised paupers into sturdy beggars to be 'scourged', while the impotent poor were to be accommodated in an almshouse.[30] Those in need of relief from outside the parish were to be removed to where they had resided for seven years or the place of their birth. Children of beggars, between 5 and 14, were to be removed and placed in the service of a person of 'good estate' and indentured until the age of 24 for males and 18 for females. A parochial poor rate was also to be levied with magistrates required to list the parish poor and to impose a tax on householders either in the form of money, food or clothing for distribution.

In 1597 administration of poor relief was transferred to the **Kirk sessions** of the Church of Scotland, funded by church collections, rental income and from fees charged for baptisms, marriages and burials.[31] Magistrates were empowered by a further Act in 1692 to erect 'houses of correction' where beggars could be offered shelter in return for work.[32]

By the start of the nineteenth century the principle of offering limited help to the able-bodied and relief only to the worthy poor had become unattainable both north and south of the Scottish border. Parochial relief was based on the assumption that the rural parish was the unit of administration but, as the Industrial Revolution gathered pace and families migrated to the major towns of Britain, it became outdated and inappropriate to meet changing needs. Furthermore, as the population expanded, the archaic assumption that work was available for all who sought it became unrealistic. Moreover, the cost of poor relief was accelerating at an alarming rate. From an estimated £600,000 in 1700, it had risen to £1.5 million by 1776 and to £4.2 million by the end of the century. Much of this was spent in supplementing the income of low wage-earners or to help out during periods of seasonal unemployment. When expenditure reached £7 million during the economic depression that followed in the wake of the Napoleonic Wars, there were increasing calls for a radical overhaul of the Poor Laws.

Chapter 4

CHARITY IN PRE-INDUSTRIAL BRITAIN

'For the recreation of poure men'
The monk Rahere, 1123

In medieval Britain there were, in theory, few uncared for poor. Work and poverty went hand in hand. As many as two-thirds of the population were serfs or villeins living a life of servitude and farming small parcels of land owned by their liege lord. Under this feudal system, which began in Saxon times and continued beyond the Norman Conquest into the sixteenth century, serfs were bound to the soil they tilled and paid their lord a tithe (or fee) for the use of his land. In return he could not dispossess his serfs without cause and was expected to support them by charity in times of hardship. It was a form of social insurance. With foodstuffs and revenue from the labour of his serfs, it made economic sense for the lord of the manor to ensure their care when unable to work or disadvantaged by old age.

The Church did the lord's work. Although incumbent upon the manorial lord, it was the Church, particularly its monasteries, that accepted responsibility for the poor and those deprived of a livelihood due to infirmity or frailty in old age. One of the tenets – indeed a cornerstone of monasticism – was the distribution of alms and every religious house was under an obligation to distribute food, clothing, medicine and money to the poor and the needy.[1] Monasteries were the oldest charitable institutions and, until they were swept away by Henry VIII in his sixteenth-century purge of Catholicism, were popular with the poor. At Glastonbury Abbey 'a large crowd' gathered at the gatehouse window for a dole of food and clothing each Wednesday and Friday, while at a monastery in Carmarthen, weekly alms were distributed to upwards of eighty people.

But monastic handouts were not available to all. By the twelfth century, canon lawyers were arguing 'we ought not to show ourselves indiscriminately generous to all who come', and cited scriptural evidence for refusing alms to the idle, since, 'if a man will not work, neither shall he eat'.[2] Taking actions that would haunt future generations of the poor, monastic communities began making the distinction between the 'deserving' or impotent poor (children, the old and the infirmed) and the 'undeserving' beggar unwilling to work.

Surviving records from a Cistercian monastery at Beaulieu in Hampshire provide an example of how charity aid was distributed. Here the almoner – a job title that continued into the twentieth century to denote the person responsible for a hospital patient's welfare – was authorised to hand out thirty pairs of shoes and the monks' old clothes to 'lepers and other paupers', and to distribute left-over bread three days each week. At harvest time, when work in the fields was plentiful, alms were not given except to pilgrims, the old, children or those incapable of work. Women, suspected of being prostitutes, were afforded alms only at times of famine.[3]

Monks had always made in-house provision for their own sick, aged and infirm brethren in a monastic farmery (from which the word infirmary is derived) but in time this provision of alms in the form of board and lodgings was extended to include the poor and aged of the lay community. The work of monasteries in offering succour to the poor and needy was recorded by one early, but unrecognised, commentator, 'they made', he wrote, 'such provision daily for the people that stood in need thereof, as sick, sore, lame, or otherwise impotent, that none or few lacked relief in one place or another. Yea, many of them, whose revenues were sufficient thereto, made hospitals and lodgings within their own houses, wherein they kept a number of impotent persons with all necessaries for them, with persons to attend to them'.[4] Moreover, the early medieval period was a time of pilgrimage, and hospitals (the name derived from the Latin *hospes*, meaning guest or stranger) also provided accommodation to wayfarers as they journeyed to religious shrines in the hope of miracle cures for disease or disability.

St John's Hospital in Winchester is probably the oldest charitable foundation in the country. This Saxon almshouse is believed to have been founded by St Brinstan, Bishop of Winchester, in AD 935. After the Norman Conquest hospitals were established throughout the country, either by religious orders or wealthy persons connected to the Church. Though disease was still thought to be the result of God's will, some employed physicians to care for the sick. Thus hospitals began to assume a dual role, that of a hostel for the frail elderly and an institution for the care of the sick. One of the earliest authenticated hospitals in Britain, the Hospital of St Peter, was founded by the canons of York Minister in AD 947. Very few survive today as solely medical establishments. One that does is St Bartholomew's in London. Affectionately known as 'Bart's', it was founded in 1123 by the monk Rahere for 'the recreation of poure men', and has continued to provide medical care on the same site for over 900 years. Some hospitals also became specialist establishments such as 'pest-houses' for contagious disease, asylums for the insane and 'lazar-houses' for victims of leprosy.

Although many were to be founded in later centuries with endowments of wealthy individuals, industrialists and philanthropic organisations, there are almshouse charities operating today that owe their existence to a medieval hospital. Unique amongst them is St Mary's Hospital in the Sussex town of Chichester, which can evidence the continuous occupation of its farmery building since about 1290. Here its current residents enjoy the comforts found within self-contained cottages built inside the framework of its original monastic structure.

The church clergy too saw it as part of their spiritual duty to relieve the suffering of the poor. In setting an example of the Church's teachings, bishops established hospitals and almshouses. In Sherburn, County Durham, Christ's Hospital, founded in 1181 by King Stephen's nephew Hugh de Puiset, Bishop of Durham, continued as a lazar-house until 1434 when it became an almshouse for the poor brethren of the parish of Thornley, although it did retain space for two lepers 'if they can be found'. In succeeding years the hospital was rebuilt and is now an active charity providing sheltered housing and respite care for the elderly. In neighbouring Yorkshire, the town of Ripon had three Church-endowed hospitals (St Mary Magdalene, St Anne's and St John the Evangelist), all of which survive, at least in part, and in their present-day guise as almshouse accommodation. They also dispensed doles of food or money. During a series of bad harvests that plagued the thirteenth century the Bishops of Winchester and Worcester gave their estate tenants a farthing a day during the difficult summers. Dispensation of a dole for the needy continues to be practised at the Hospital of St Cross in Winchester. Founded in 1130 by Bishop Henry de Blois as an almshouse 'for thirteen poor men, feeble and so reduced in strength that they can scarcely or not at all support themselves without aid',[5] travellers can still, in the twenty-first century, request a 'wayfarer's dole', consisting of bread and a mug of ale or beer. Lower down the Church hierarchy, with money received from tithe income,

Beamsley Hospital. Founded by Margaret, Countess of Cumberland in 1593, Beamsley Hospital originally housed seven poor widows, one of whom was appointed 'mother' and the other six as 'sisters'. The latter had one tiny bedroom each, as well as a living room for the mother, with a chapel at its centre. After Margaret's death in 1616 her daughter, Lady Anne Clifford, was said to have 'erected the greatest part of the said hospital' by building a row of six dwellings alongside, thereby achieving her late mother's wish that the endowment should be for thirteen poor widows of Skipton. The Hospital's income came from the rent of two farms that kept the buildings in repair and paid an allowance to the inmates. In 1983 the trustees passed the buildings to The Landmark Trust which, after restoration, let the newer properties to permanent tenants, while the round building (seen here) is let to parties of up to five for holidays. For details: telephone 0162 882 5920; website: www.landmarktrust.org.uk. (Reproduced by permission of The Landmark Trust)

charitable works were undertaken at parish level. Although by 1391 this provision of care was found wanting and necessitated government intervention when the Appropriation of Benefices Act reminded parish rectors to spend their income wisely 'for poor parishioners of the churches to help their life and sustenance at all times'. The Church congregation too made donations to charity but, in these heady religious times, it was often driven more by personal indulgence.

Helping the poor was an opportunity for wealthy donors to ensure their own salvation. Testators left money for priests to say mass for their souls, often in purpose-built chapels or chantries and for food, clothing or money to be distributed to the poor at their funeral. Wakes of the wealthy were popular. In 1489, over 13,000 poor people are reported to have received a two-penny dole at the funeral of the 4th Earl of Northumberland.[6] Religious motives were also behind the founding of bedehouses, where pauper residents, known as bedesmen or bedeswomen, spent their lives in grateful prayer for their benefactor's soul.

Those who could ill afford to provide for a chantry, let alone a decent burial, banded together to form fraternities, otherwise known as parish guilds. They were principally burial clubs providing for a decent internment and for prayers to be said for their members' souls. Members paid a 'mass penny' for the upkeep of the altar and the payment of a priest and were expected to bequeath an amount of their worldly goods to guild funds – 1s for every pound's worth of chattels, up to a maximum of 40s, in the case of the Guild of St Mary and the Holy Cross in Chesterfield – as well as an annual collection of alms for the poor. In 1520, St Mary's guild in the Lincolnshire town of Boston had an income of £900 (a sum worth around £341,622 today). The larger guilds, with handsome endowments from wealthy benefactors and regular subscriptions from hundreds of members, were able to build elegant guildhalls for the purposes of trade, homes for destitute members and almshouses for the aged poor. Their members often dominated local civic administration and, after the suppression of the guilds in the sixteenth century, went on to form the nuclei of town councils. They made individual benefactions too. Thomas Bond, mayor of Coventry in 1497, and a member of the city's Holy Trinity fraternity, bequeathed sufficient funds in his will to build a hospital 'for the care and maintenance of ten poor men'.[7] In 1832, Bond's Hospital was restored and by 1940 such was the income from his endowment that eighty-five almsmen were being provided with 6s a week.

The succession of Henry VIII to the throne in 1509 led to a period of turmoil for the monarchy and its people; for the poor amongst them it was the precursor to the removal of a cornerstone of charitable relief. Henry's failure to win the support of the Pope for his divorce from Catherine of Aragon led him to break away from the Catholic Church and appoint himself Protector and Supreme Head of a new Church of England. What followed was a root and branch purge of Catholicism throughout the towns and shires, including the greatest plunder of Church property ever seen in England: the dissolution of monasteries.

In 1533, according to the *Valor Ecclesiasticus* survey undertaken by Henry's Chancellor of the Exchequer, Thomas Cromwell, there were 500 monasteries, 163 nunneries and a scattering of Franciscan, Dominican and Augustinian friaries in England and Wales that considered it part of religious life to succour the poor and the suffering. But there were elements within these monastic communities who had left themselves open to criticism when they were found to be idle and immoral. Frequently ignoring their vows of poverty and chastity, many enjoyed a standard of living in excess of their contemporaries and certainly that of the old, the sick and the poor whom they were supposed to help. This laxity encouraged Henry to close the smaller monasteries in 1536, but it was only a prelude to wholesale closure and within four years the dissolution of the monasteries was complete.

The Church was cleansed of remaining popish influence in 1546 when the Chantries Act suppressed religious fraternities and allowed the Crown to confiscate chantries that had 'superstitious and childish observations' and were not wholly for charitable purposes. According to the Act's preamble, appropriated monies were to be put to 'good and godly use' in the erection of schools and a better provision for the poor and destitute. In the event, few schools were founded or almshouse built using these sequestered funds; the cost of the latest war with France saw to that.

The dissolution of the monasteries, the suppression of religious fraternities and the confiscation of chantries radically reduced existing sources of charity. Estimates suggest monasteries alone dispensed £6,500 a year in alms to the poor and the destitute in hard times.[8] The removal of this resource was one of the factors in the creation of an army of 'sturdy beggars' that plagued England from the mid-sixteenth century that led to the enactment of the Edwardian and Elizabethan Poor Laws. Monasteries had been important employers too and the nation's poor were augmented by a disbanded religious community, most of whom were impoverished themselves. While some were pensioned off or offered bishoprics in the cathedrals of the new Church of England, an estimated 6,500 friars, monks, canons and nuns were thrown onto the labour market, but a significantly higher number were the lay people employed by the monasteries. For example, eight yeomen and twenty-six servants employed at a nunnery in Polesworth, Warwickshire found themselves without home or work.

Many hospitals however, whether in the form of almshouses for the aged or medical institutions for the sick, survived due to the actions of municipalities or benevolent groups and individuals. The mayor and aldermen of the City of London petitioned the king to refound hospitals for the sick that 'were not like other houses for the maintenance of priests, canons and clerks living carnally as they had done lately'.[9] As a result, five royal, or chartered, hospitals were re-established in the city – St Bartholomew's Hospital (1546) and St Thomas's Hospital (1551) for the physically infirm, St Mary's Bethlem (1546) as a lunatic asylum, the Bridewell (1552), a prison reformatory, and Christ's Hospital (1553) as a refuge for orphaned children. Examples in the provinces included the burgesses of Poole in Dorset who bought back from the Crown a hospital founded by the Corpus Christi Guild, and in Abingdon, diplomat and Member of Parliament John Mason purchased the dissolved St Helen's Guild Hospital, founded in 1442 to house seven poor men and six women, which survives today in this Oxfordshire town as part of a complex known as the Long Alley Almshouse.

Tudor governments did not expect the statutory system of poor relief to replace wholly the loss of alms from religious sources. They intended that the poor should only receive state aid determined under the Poor Laws when levels of poverty exceeded the capacity of private philanthropy. Tudor administrators looked therefore to the private charity sector to produce most of the funds. The voluntary provision of social welfare was already well established by the mid-sixteenth century. According to W K Jordan, over £472,000 (around £95 million today) had been raised in charitable benefactions since the start of the century.[10] This funded such diverse projects as the better treatment for prisoners, particularly those incarcerated for debt, public works such as municipal road repairs, the founding of grammar schools for the better off and hospitals to care for both rich and poor. However, by far the most significant single concern for private charitable donors was in the relief of poverty.

Born out of a fear of social disorder and with 'a sense of national conscience and national obligation [and] a pervasive desire to emulate the charitable acts of others . . .' all social groups able to pay – peers and gentry, higher and lower clergy, merchants and traders, yeomen and husbandmen – contributed increasing sums to alleviate the plight of the poor.[11] As a result of this outpouring of charitable wealth the relief of poverty by the end of the sixteenth century was being borne by the benevolence of individual citizens or caring organisations, rather than the state system. Not until the early eighteenth century, when urbanisation and industrialisation began to impact on the nation and introduce changing patterns of need, did income from the poor rate surpass the value of private charitable donations. Jordan calculates that between 1480 and 1660 over £3 million was raised from charitable sources – a third of which was expended on the poor, either in outright relief or in areas of social rehabilitation.[12] To give something to a worthy cause – relief of the poor, prison reform, an almshouse for the elderly or a school or hospital – came to be expected in Tudor and Elizabethan society. Even after death the failure of a wealthy testator to settle a gift to charity was considered shocking.

The government actively encouraged such charitable activities. They were determined to provide safeguards for an expanding system of charitable relief and ensure funds raised from private sources were properly and legally managed. In 1597 an 'Act to reforme Deceits and Breaching of Trust, touching lands given to Charitable Uses' was enacted. This was refined and amplified in 1601 by a second Act that became more commonly known as the 'Statute of Charitable Uses' and would remain fundamental to charity law, until its repeal in the twentieth century. In a practical way it authorised the Lord Chancellor to appoint commissioners to inquire into charitable activities, investigate complaints and establish whether the terms of a bequest were being satisfied.

By far the most significant charitable sums throughout the Elizabethan and Stuart periods came from members of the mercantile community. Of the £121,800 raised from all charitable sources between 1561 and 1660, over £68,000 came from the philanthropy of merchants. Such was the extent of their combined contributions that, by the end of the sixteenth century, merchants were providing succour to six out of every ten paupers. There were two purposes above all that attracted their wealth: the 'outright relief' for the poor in cash, clothing or food; and almshouses for deserving paupers who were past their useful labour.

It was the road to personal salvation that led merchants and traders of sixteenth-century Britain to help the poor. They fulfilled their obligation to society and the hereafter by bequeathing money, from a few pounds to vast fortunes, or by leaving instructions for the establishment of a charitable trust. **Parochial charities** were set up and money disbursed by trustees (often the local clergy) to assist the able-bodied poor in their own homes. This was in the form of household relief and paid until employment could be found or illness cured. Created by benefactors as a lasting and socially worthy memorial, there was often little sentiment with such a provision. The levels of payment in these bequests, often stipulated by the testator – which also placed a useful means of social control in the hands of the clergy and local dignitaries – were intended to do no more than keep a family from starvation and abject want. In Yorkshire, an average £2 a year was awarded to destitute families, in London it was £2 15s, while in Worcestershire, £2 16s was paid out.[13] Although these funds were unevenly distributed across the country, there existence ensured poverty never got out of hand and the poor were maintained at manageable levels. When the charities' funds were inadequate to meet demand (for example, the acute hardship created by a series of disastrous harvests that devastated the country in the 1590s), overseers resorted to doling out Poor Law relief, but this was regarded only as a temporary measure and trustees returned to disbursing parochial funds as soon as they were able to do so.

By the early seventeenth century, there was a move away from funding outright relief towards a greater emphasis on the foundation of almshouses. Benefactors became more discriminatory when a statutory system of poor relief was in place that met basic needs. It was also borne out of a determination to avoid helping the hoards of disreputable and disorderly 'rogues, vagrants and vagabonds' that were plaguing the country. Furthermore, philanthropists were encouraged to found and endow almshouses by a simplification of the legal process. In 1572, the Hospitals for the Poor Act was introduced to assist those who wished to found hospitals and almshouses. Twenty-five years later, under the Elizabethan Poor Law of 1597, it became no longer necessary to obtain royal consent or an individual Act of Parliament before 'erecting hospitals or abiding and working houses for the poor', which could instead be effected by a 'deede inrolled [sic] in the High Court of Chancery'.

In the seventeenth century, over 220 charities with resident accommodation had been founded, compared with only 55 a century before. One of the earliest almshouses of the century was Jesus Hospital in the Berkshire village of Bray. It was founded by William Goddard in 1609 for forty poor people, six of whom, he stipulated in his will, were to be freemen of the Fishmongers' Company. Amongst those who followed his lead was Richard Wyatt, a successful timber merchant and three times Master of the Carpenters' Company, who, in 1619, bequeathed funds to build almshouses in Godalming for 'the deserving poor'. James Lancaster, a founder member of the Skinners' Company, also left his wealth to the poor. As too did Martin Bowes, a Yorkshire goldsmith, but outstripping them all was the Lincolnshire merchant Thomas Sutton. Having made his fortune from coal mining in the north of England, his good deeds included the founding of London Charterhouse School and Sutton Hospital for eighty poor men who were to be impoverished gentlemen, old soldiers and sailors, merchants whose livelihood had been lost due to piracy or shipwreck and royal servants. After his death in 1611, having catered for the poor of his home parish, the residue £50,000 of his fortune (worth £4.8 million today) was added to the endowment of his hospital.

Merchants were not concerned solely with the maintenance of the poor or the provision of almshouses. They also supported the allied problems of social rehabilitation. Funds were made available for artisans in temporary financial difficulties lest they might easily become progressively poorer; endowments were provided for apprenticeships; and stocks of materials purchased for use by the poor in workhouses on work-related activities.

The gentry and the aristocracy were also helping the poor. When Edward Stafford, the 3rd Duke of Buckingham, was executed for treason on 16 May 1521, the assembled crowd were fed 'a great fat oxe . . . with bread and drinke aboundantly [sic] . . . and everyone had in addition a dole of 2d'.[14] And sixty years later between 3,000 and 4,000 poor were fed the leftovers from the wake of Edward, Earl of Rutland, and over a 1,000 were similarly treated at the feast of Lady Berkeley in 1596.[15] Lord Burleigh built almshouses on his Lincolnshire estate, and in Yorkshire, Margaret, Countess of Cumberland, founded Beamsley Hospital in 1593 for thirteen poor widows, after she found 'many old women in and around Skipton decrepit and broken down by old age, who were in the habit of begging for their daily bread'.

For some, the very act of giving was its own reward, and gave indiscriminately in their lifetime to the poor – in the street, in the

The Rules of Beamsley Hospital, 1665

1. That Prayer be daily said everie morning about Eight or Nyne a Clock by the Reader for the tyme being. And that the mother and all the Twelve sisters give their constant attendance at the said Prayers and none of them to be absent at any tyme unless in Cases of Sickness or other urgent occasions.

2. That none of the Sisters be out of the house without the leave of the Reader who prayeth with them and the mother of the said Almshouse.

3. That none of their children or grandchildren or any other shall lye with sisters in the said Almshouse without the leave of the said Reader or mother whych leave shall not be granted but only in Case of Sickness or other Reasonable occasion.

4. That the out doors of the Almshouse may be constantly locked up everie night at Eight a Clock in winter and Nyne in the somer and not to be opened in the morning till Seven a Clock in the winter and Six in the somer.

5. That none of the Sisters do Run on the Score of the Towne because they have their allowance paid them constantly.

6. That the Almshouse court be swept over everie week, and the runnels and watercourses about it kept clean.

7. That the mother also herself observe these orders.

8. That the mother and Sisters do all of them Indevour to live peaceably and quiet among themselves.

9. That if any difference shall arise amongst any of the Sisters or mother and Sisters, It may be determined between the Major Part themselves and the Reader, and in the case they cannot end Itt then to be refered to the Countess of Pembroke while she liveth and after her death such differences to be refered to the owner of Skipton Castle for the time being.

10. That if the mother or any of the Twelve Sisters shall wilfully break any of these orders that for first fault they shall forfeit a fortnights Allowance to be abated out of the next moneys they are to Receive, and equally divided one half to the Informer and the other half to the poor of the Towne, and for the second fault to be expelled from the house.

11. When any other is to succeed in the house they shall submit to these orders or else they shall not be admitted.

(Reproduced by permission of The Landmark Trust)

tavern yard or at the church gate. Most of these spontaneous acts by their very nature went unrecorded, but the accounts of Cumberland landowner and merchant Christopher Lowther reveal his gifts in the early seventeenth century: '1 /2d to "a poor man", 4d to "a poor man at church", and 1s to "the poor on Easter Sunday"'.[16] For the poor, unrehearsed acts of generosity could be rich pickings: in mid-sixteenth-century Norwich a poor woman had £44 (around £8,800 today) on her when she was apprehended for begging.

Nicholas Chamberlaine Almshouse, Bedworth, Warwickshire. Born to a wealthy family in 1632, Nicholas Chamberlaine became rector of the Warwickshire village of Bedworth in the early 1660s. As a widower with no children, he left his wealth for the benefit of the poor of the parish. In his will, Chamberlaine appointed trustees to undertake his wishes and build an almshouse for twelve women and six men of the Anglican faith. The almshouse was rebuilt in an Elizabethan style in 1840 at a cost of £9,000. With Housing Association and English Heritage grants, a comprehensive refurbishment programme has now converted the building into twenty-seven flats, with communal areas and a full-time warden, while the Grade II listed exterior has been restored to its former glory. It is still a very local amenity; many of the current residents' parents and grandparents had previously lived there. (Reproduced by permission of the Bedworth Society)

There were innumerable acts of individual generosity. Citizens kept 'poor boxes', as Samuel Pepys did, and so too did the Church, when the clergy also encouraged their congregation to fast on a Friday and give bread to the poor. In the late eighteenth century, Evangelical Member of Parliament William Wilberforce regularly donated a quarter of his income to charitable causes and supported over seventy philanthropic organisations. One of which was the Society for Bettering the Condition of the Poor, founded by the lawyer and philanthropist Sir Thomas Bernard which by 1811 had raised over £15,000.

There were also a range of local eccentric initiatives too. In Cheshire, cow charities were once common when cattle were rented out at low

Dartford Charity School

In 1745 the Revd Charles Chambres, vicar of Dartford, bequeathed £25 to the churchwardens of Holy Trinity church to be invested. Income from this investment was to be used to pay for an annual sermon aimed at encouraging the parishioners to establish and fund, by subscription, a new Charity School in Dartford.

The terms of the will dictated that, following the preaching of the annual sermon, the churchwardens should stand with collection plates at the church doors to receive the gifts of the congregation. It took three years for the Charity School to be established. The school was initially held in the north chancel of Holy Trinity Church, St Thomas' Chapel, but later moved to the vestry.

The vicar and churchwardens played an active part in selecting as many poor children as the money allowed to receive a basic education. Some of the Charity School pupils were recruited direct from the workhouse.

The success of the new venture depended on a reliable and regular source of funding. Voluntary subscriptions were received from local parishioners on an annual basis. Additional funding was secured from bequests. In 1771 John Randall bequeathed £100 'to be put out to interest, for schooling and clothing as many poor boys as the interest would admit'. In 1778, Catherine Tasker bequeathed £50 for promoting and encouraging the Charity School and in 1795 Mary Pettit bequeathed £1,000, the interest from which was to be given to the Charity School at Dartford.

By the end of the eighteenth century, both boys and girls were being taught at the church-based Charity School. The Charity School merged with the Sunday school in 1816.

(Reproduced by permission of the Dartford Town Archive)

rates to 'poor and godly parishioners'. At Alresford in Essex, the milk from two cows was given to the poor each morning between Whitsun and Michaelmas (29 September). At Retford, a field on the outskirts of this Nottingham town was let rent free to anyone willing to take charge of its resident bull, available to service the cows of poorer parishioners.[17]

Charity also extended to educating poor children. With money raised by subscription from church congregations, the Society for Propagating Christian Knowledge (SPCK) was founded in 1699. Its first school was St George's in the London district of Southwark and by 1729 there were 132 schools scattered throughout the country with 5,225 pupils aged between 7 and 12. Some only admitted children of the 'respectable poor', while others gave priority to the poorest. Ill-disciplined children 'who were not real objects of charity' were refused admission and schools often boarded their pupils for fear that family life would undermine school discipline. It was intended that all children should emerge as industrious and sober 'hewers of wood and drawers of water', and uniforms were intentionally dull to discourage vanity.[18] Boys were trained to become apprentices in humble occupations and girls made ready for a life of domestic service.

Another example of **schools for the poor** that have an earlier history and were founded by charitable endowments is the bluecoat school. The first, with its distinctive cassock-like, blue uniform – the favoured colour for charity schools in Tudor times when blue was the cheapest dye available and also implied humble status – was Christ's Hospital in the City of London. Over the centuries nearly eighty schools imitated the dress code to become bluecoat schools. Many survive and one that celebrated its tercentenary in 2008 is the Liverpool Blue Coat School. Opened as an institution and dedicated to the promotion of Christian charity for the training of poor boys, it retained its orphanage role until 1940, by which time it had moved to larger premises in once-rural Wavertree on the outskirts of the city.

Chapter 5

POOR LAWS IN THE NINETEENTH CENTURY

'Every penny bestowed, that tends to render the condition of the
pauper more eligible than that of the independent labourer, is a
bounty on indolence and vice'.
Report of the Poor Law Commission, 1834

In 1832 the government agreed to establish a Royal Commission to
inquire into the Poor Laws; a decision motivated not only by long-
term concerns about the operation of the laws but also, since the
end of the Napoleonic Wars in 1815, the spiralling cost of poor relief.
Ratepayers had generally accepted that a higher poor rate was
necessary during the war years to protect the poor in a time of crisis,
but the expected reduction did not materialise in peacetime. In the
depressed economy of the immediate post-war period the total cost of
poor relief rose from £5.7 million in 1815 to peak at £7.9 million by
1817. Although this gradually fell back as the economy recovered in
succeeding years, a series of bad harvests in the 1820s, producing a
shortage of work and agricultural distress, resulted in a rise in the cost
of poor relief every year from 1823, to reach £7 million again by 1831.

There were also concerns about the maladministration of poor relief
funds by parish overseers. Contracts to supply food for the poor or
workhouse materials and services were routinely awarded to local
tradesmen rather than by open tender. There were also cases where
inadequate supervision in distributing poor relief had led to it being
inappropriately spent. 'Hundreds of instances,' reported one parish
elder, giving evidence to the Commission, 'came under my
observation, in which the Overseer knew that the parish allowance was
spent in two nights at the beer'.[1] Echoing these concerns, the Sturges
Bourne's Acts of 1818 and 1819 allowed parishes to establish small
committees, or Select Vestries, headed by a salaried assistant overseer,

to take administration of poor relief out of the hands of the Open Vestry, scrutinise relief-giving and put it on a more professional footing.[2]

The third area of concern was based on the contemporary view of the poor and their perceived behaviour. There was a growing sentiment that poverty was not the result of unemployment, high prices or other social and economic factors, but rather, that the poor brought hardship on themselves through idleness, fecklessness and above all moral failings. Furthermore, commentators and ratepayers alike argued the Speenhamland ruling of 1795, linking agricultural wages to inflation – already placing an intolerable burden on those responsible for raising the poor rate – demoralised the workforce in offering little incentive to work when the parish could be expected to meet their needs. Moreover, farmers get away with not paying full wages when cheap, parish-subsidised labour was available.

The fourth point was that the old Poor Law did not provide a standardised and nationwide system of welfare benefits. Provision varied across the country, in some areas the care of the sick and elderly was totally inadequate and in many parishes the level of support afforded to out of work labourers was barely enough to avoid starvation and ensure survival. But they reflected a tradition in which the better off members of society accepted some responsibility for the welfare of the poorest. As such, the early Poor Laws were regarded by the poor as a safety net in times of hardship and from which they had the right to benefit. It was this notion of a 'right' that came under increasing attack at the start of the nineteenth century.

From the 1790s onwards some of the most prominent social commentators were putting forward their own schemes for the relief of the poor. Amongst them was the philosopher and writer Jeremy Bentham. In his book *Pauper Management Improved* (1798), Bentham proposed giving responsibility for the poor to a body to be known as the National Charity Organisation. Under this scheme all forms of outdoor relief would be abolished and 'houses of industry' provided for the poor. Life within the houses would be deliberately hard with long working hours and meagre diets. In what would eventually resurface as the 'workhouse test' in the middle of the next century, conditions were designed to be less desirable than those outside so as to deter all but the most desperate from entering. Indeed, many of Bentham's proposals, of centralised administration, economic efficiency and minimum universal standards, were influential when the commissioners came to look at the Poor Laws: crucially, Bentham's one-time secretary, Edwin Chadwick – a dominant force behind the 1832 inquiry – was himself a committed 'Benthamite'.

Also holding radical views that would ultimately influence the Commission's inquiry was parson and writer Thomas Malthus. In his *Essay on Population* (1796), Malthus expanded on his theory that the expansion of the population, so noticeable at the time, would eventually outstrip available food supplies. If the population continued to grow, he reasoned, widespread famine and disaster would surely follow. He justified his case by blaming the Poor Laws:

> The labouring poor to use a common expression seem always to live from hand to mouth. Their present wants employ their whole attention, and they seldom think of the future. Even when they have an opportunity for saving they seldom exercise it, but all that is beyond their present necessities goes, generally speaking, to the ale-house. The Poor Laws of England may therefore be said to diminish both the power and the will to save among the common people, and thus to weaken one of the strongest incentives to sobriety and industry, and consequently happiness.[3]

Malthus called for the total abolition of the Poor Laws, arguing that, relieved of the burden of the poor rate, landowners and employers would be able to pay higher rates of pay. It would also lead, in Malthus's view, to smaller families because the incentive to have more children simply to get more poor relief would be removed.

There was unrest too amongst the labouring classes. Faced with the threat of mechanisation, farm labourers rebelled. Riots, led by the shadowy Captain Swing, started in Kent and spread throughout much of southern England when hayricks were burned, buildings razed and threshing machines destroyed. Workhouses and other symbols of the much-despised Poor Laws were also attacked. The government took strong action to quell the riots. Troops were dispatched to areas of disturbance and rewards offered that led to the capture of the rioters. With France suffering political turmoil and the fear of revolution in Britain real, the civil disturbances proved to be the final crisis of the old Poor Laws and the catalyst that precipitated change.

The Royal Commission on the Poor Laws, consisting ultimately of nine commissioners, was established 'to make a diligent and full inquiry into the practical operation of the laws for the relief of the poor in England and Wales . . . and to report whether any, and what,

Attack on the workhouse. Stockport Poor Law Union Workhouse was erected in 1841 and soon after opening there was a widespread manufacturing slump that led to riots in northern areas, when the unemployed rebelled against the new Poor Laws. In August 1842 'upwards of 20,000 persons out of employment in this place who had no resources but those of plunder and beggary' attacked the Stockport workhouse. A government force, composed of constables and a detachment of the Cheshire Yeomanry, was dispatched to quell the rioters – but not before they had requisitioned '672 seven-pound loaves and a considerable quantity of copper coins'. (Reproduced by permission of George C Landow, Brown University, Rhode Island, United States of America)

alterations, amendments or improvements may be beneficially made in the said laws'. Alongside lawyer turned civil servant Edwin Chadwick, the other influential member of the Commission was Nassau Senior, appointed for his experience in having reported extensively on the poor in Ireland. He maintained the unorthodox view for the time that chronic poverty should not be met simply by relieving the worst cases of social distress, but by improvements in industrial productivity, which in turn would enhance the moral character and lift the poor out of their misery. 'Workers should accept any job the market offered regardless of the working conditions or pay. Any person who would not or could not find work should be given just enough [relief] to prevent physical starvation', he argued.[4] Chadwick shared similar views and between them they became the main architects of the Commission's Report.

Under the influence of Senior and Chadwick, twenty-six assistant commissioners were employed to collect information and assess the operation of the Poor Laws. They were expected to establish two basic principles: that outdoor relief was economically unsustainable and demoralised the labouring classes, and that the only obvious alternative, the workhouse, was inefficient when left to individual parishes to manage. To achieve these aims they were to interview the parish clergy, overseers and magistrates, cross-examine witnesses, attend vestry meetings and inspect documentation. In what was the first national survey of its kind, 3,000 of the 15,000 parishes and townships in England and Wales were investigated. Given the political ideologies of Senior and Chadwick, the methodology was driven as much by economic efficiency as by the need to help the poor. Moreover, historians argue, they came to their conclusions at the outset of the investigation and intended to use the findings only as a tool to reform the Poor Laws in the fashion they had already chosen.[5] One testimony the inquiry team included as 'an instructive example of the tendency of pauperism to sap the foundations of industry, virtue and happiness' was supplied by a Mr Sleeth of Kent Road, London: 'I have been witness to the gradual ruin of a very deserving class of people, effected, as well as I can judge, by the superior temptations of parish allowance and idleness, to those of independence with industry'.[6] In another, a Mr Booker, described as a resident in the western division of the Metropolis, commented, 'the deterioration in the character and habits of persons receiving parochial relief, pervade their whole conduct; they become idle, reckless and saucy; and if we take them into the [poor] house the younger learn from the older and all their malpractices, and are ready enough to follow'.[7]

When the Poor Law Commission's Report was published in March 1834 it took the view that poverty was essentially caused by idleness and indolence, rather than by lack of work or the result of other social and economic factors. In a damming indictment of the old Poor Laws, it concluded that paupers were able to claim poor relief regardless of their merits. Improvident marriages had increased; immorality was encouraged, when women claimed relief for their bastard offspring; large families got most; and labourers had little incentive to work, when employers kept wages artificially low in the knowledge that they would be subsidised from the poor rates. 'Can we wonder', the authors noted, 'if the uneducated are seduced into approving a system which aims its allurements at the weakest parts of our nature – which offers marriage to the young, security to the anxious, ease to the lazy and impunity to the profligate'.[8]

It was essential, the Report claimed, that a clearer distinction was made between the able-bodied labourer and the impotent 'worthy' poor.

> Throughout the evidence it is shown, that in proportion as the condition of any pauper class is elevated above the condition of independent labourers, the condition of the independent class is depressed; their industry is impaired, their employment becomes unsteady, and its remuneration in wages is diminished. Such persons, therefore, are under the strongest inducements to quit the less eligible class of labourers and enter the more eligible class of paupers . . . every penny bestowed, that tends to render the condition of the pauper more eligible than that of the independent labourer, is a bounty on indolence and vice. We have found, that as the poor rates are at present administered, they operate as bounties of this description, to the amount of several million annually.[9]

The commissioners recommended that the Poor Law system should be administered by locally appointed boards, under the direction of a central authority. At the heart of the system would be the workhouse to 'relieve the helpless, deter the idle, set children on the right path, encourage thrift and temperance, reduce crime, improve agriculture, raise wages and heal the growing divisions in the social order'.[10] In a measure to assuage those who considered poor relief encouraged 'idleness and recklessness that threatened the stability and respectability of society',[11] all relief to the able-bodied and their families, other than that supplied in the workhouse, should be abolished entirely. The old Poor Laws had imposed a heavy burden on small impoverished parishes that had a poor economy and in turn were likely to have a greater number of paupers in their midst. Parishes in these areas should therefore be encouraged to combine to provide a shared workhouse under the auspices of a Poor Law union.

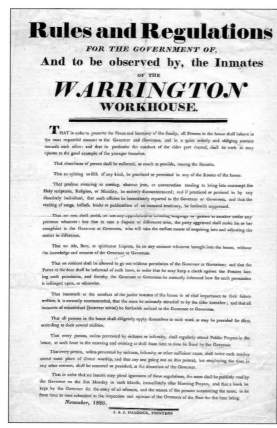

Warrington workhouse rules, 1820. Warrington's first workhouse was erected in 1728 and accommodated 100 inmates. The rules of the house included the barring of alcohol, no spitting or filth of any kind, no profane swearing, cursing or 'obscene jests'. There was also a ban on the 'reading of songs, ballads, books or publications of an immoral tendency'. After a Poor Law union was established this was replaced in 1851 by the larger, and perhaps inappropriately named, Lovely Lane Workhouse. (Reproduced by permission of Warrington Borough Council, Libraries, Heritage & Learning)

The Report also recommended the workhouse separation of paupers into four different classes: the aged and sick, children, able-bodied males and able-bodied females. Segregating paupers, it was believed, would enable each group to be properly catered for; treatment, care and rest for the sick and the elderly, education for the children and the able-bodied put to work. As later years would prove, this was too simplistic a separation. In practice, workhouses, unable to afford to employ dedicated staff, would require inmates to care for the sick or educate the children and ignored these rules of separation. It did not take account of the infectious, the slightly mad or the infant at the breast. Neither did it make separate provision for the roaming vagrant, the prostitute or the petty criminal, who at times were to find themselves in the workhouse, either voluntarily or by committal.

Although illness was one of the major contributory factors of poverty, it received little attention in the Report. Under the old Poor Laws, parishes sought the agreement of a local physician who, on payment of an annual retainer, attended to any sick pauper. With all poor relief now envisaged to be provided by the workhouse, Boards of Governors were to appoint Medical Officers and workhouse masters to decide whether or not the sick were entitled to medical treatment. The result of this arrangement saw medical relief kept to a minimum: in 1840 when total expenditure on Poor Law relief was £4.5 million, only £150,000 went on medical services.[12]

The government responded to the Royal Commission's Report in 1834 with the enactment of the Act for the Amendment and better Administration of the Laws relating to the Poor in England and Wales. This brought about a radical reform to the system of poor relief in England and Wales. In adopting all of the Report's key recommendations, the Act provided for: the establishment of a central authority to regulate and monitor the implementation of the Poor Law; the grouping together of parishes to create Poor Law unions; the construction of workhouses in each union; and a proposal to at first restrict and then abolish all 'outdoor relief' for the able-bodied poor.

The introduction of the Poor Law Amendment Act was greeted with widespread hostility and failed in its immediate attempts to establish a new system of poor relief. The parish remained the orbit of most people's lives and there was resentment at the bureaucratic intrusion of central government into local affairs. Overseers and parish officials not only felt they were best able to manage their own poor but also recognised the advantage to ratepayers when outdoor relief was a more cost-effective option than providing workhouse indoor relief. The poor themselves feared the prospect of family separation in the harsh, prison-like regime of the new workhouse where poverty, more than ever, would be punished as a crime.

The parish workhouse, established under the 'old' laws and accommodating chiefly old people, women and children, had enjoyed considerable freedom by offering simple, but adequate, respite: now that image was to change. In order to discourage applicants, living conditions were designed to be deliberately inferior to those of the gainfully employed so as to act as a deterrent and ensure only 'deserving cases' were admitted. To achieve this aim, the workhouse test was revived in the belief that anyone prepared to accept workhouse relief must be lacking the moral determination to survive without it. With the government's intention to abolish outdoor relief for all but the elderly and infirm, those who failed this 'principle of less eligibility' would have no entitlement to poor relief.

An alternative to the workhouse was **emigration** and the Act permitted Boards of Guardians to supply money, clothing or goods to poor families to aid them in their passage to the colonies. Although there was some reluctance on the part of colonial administrators to receive paupers who were down on their luck or perceived as 'workshy', overseas settlement assistance continued until the late nineteenth century. Between 1836 and 1846 alone over 14,000 families took advantage of the scheme and emigrated to an uncertain future in an unknown overseas British territory. Included in this number were two families from the Sussex town of Battle where entries in the vestry minutes include: '11 Feb 1841 . . . to pay expenses of James Eldridge, wife and 3 children to Australia not exceeding twenty pounds' and on the '18 Mar 1841 . . . to advance William Gibbs and family of 5 children, twenty-five pounds to assist him to emigrate to Canada'.[13]

The central authority established by the Act was the Poor Law Commission and one of its first tasks was the creation of new Poor Law unions. Under the 'old' Poor Laws each of the 15,000 parishes in England and Wales was responsible for the poor in its own area. Now the aim was to amalgamate parishes into groups each managed by a Board of Guardians comprising representatives from each participating parish.

The process of creating unions was slow and varied across the country. Assistant commissioners, without powers of enforcement, had to rely on persuasion to encourage parishes to comply. To achieve this, consultation with local communities was required and public meetings held for the purpose. Contemporary newspaper accounts suggest this was a troublesome task. The *Derby Mercury* featured the following report in January 1837:

> Mr Stevens, the Assistant Poor Law Commissioner, met some of the ratepayers and magistrates of Derby on Tuesday at the Town Hall for the purpose of forming that town and the villages within three miles of it into a union under the Poor Law Act. After a lengthened discussion, part of the commissioner's petition was rejected, and in conformity with the views of those present, the union was confined to the five parishes of Derby.[14]

The commissioners were under additional pressure to get results

Abingdon workhouse, Oxfordshire. Abingdon Poor Law Union was formed in
January 1835 and was the first union to be declared under the Poor Law
(Amendment) Act. By October of that year it represented thirty-eight parishes
scattered throughout rural Berkshire and neighbouring Oxfordshire. The earliest
workhouse in Abingdon dates from 1631, but in 1835 a new workhouse (seen here)
was built to accommodate 500 residents at a total cost of £9,000. Its hexagonal
layout enabled the separation of men, women, boys and girls irrespective of any
family relationship. The land adjoining the rear of the workhouse was turned over
to growing vegetables and pigs were kept in a piggery. The workhouse, known
locally as the 'Grubber', continued to operate until 1932 when its patients were
transferred to nearby Wallingford. A detailed history of Abingdon workhouse,
together with a list of nineteenth-century staff and residents, can be found at:
www.workhouses.org.uk/. (Reproduced by permission of Simon Fowler)

when unions were also intended to undertake the registration of births,
marriages and deaths, which was due to commence in 1837. According
to the correspondent of a January 1837 edition of the *Stockport Advertiser*:

> Mr Coppock, the Assistant Poor Law Commissioner, met with
> ratepayers of Stockport for the purpose of naming guardians
> under the new Poor Law Act, only (as he assured them) for

carrying out the provisions of the Registration of Births &c, Act. In answer to several questions put to him, Mr Coppock said that men of 60 and their wives would not in future be separated [in the workhouse] without their consent, but young men and their wives would be. After a very stormy discussion, in the course of which the new Poor Law Act was unmercifully abused, as well as the administrators of it, two nominal guardians, one chosen by those on the platform, and one by the meeting, were appointed.[15]

The commissioners also had to contend with the 'Gilbert Unions'. These were districts that had already amalgamated for poor-relief purposes under the Act of 1782. There were also parishes that had established local Poor Law committees under the Sturges Bourne Acts. Both of these were outside the control of the Poor Law Commission and its assistant commissioners were required to work around these areas when planning a new Poor Law union.

Even when a new union had been established the commissioners faced a second difficulty. Although they could require the alteration of an existing workhouse, they had no powers to order the building of a new one. This could only be undertaken if the majority of the members of the newly appointed local Board of Guardians voted for one. With representatives from each participating parish on the board, parishes with very few poor could hold back a minority of parishes in the union with larger numbers of poor residents. At Bradford in Yorkshire, for example, the predominantly rural parishes vetoed proposals of the inner townships to build a union workhouse.

The poor themselves also rebelled against the 'new' Poor Law. Most hated of all were the 'workhouse test' and the severe restrictions imposed on the payment of outdoor relief. In the south of England riots were witnessed in Buckinghamshire when, in May 1835, a mob took to the streets in an attempt to prevent paupers being moved from their home parish of Chesham to a new, grim and distant workhouse in Amersham. Similar incidents occurred in Kent and Norfolk before spreading throughout much of rural England. Yet, 6 years after the Act reached the statute books, despite initial difficulties, 14,000 parishes, with a total population of 12 million, had been incorporated into Poor Law unions. Most of the 350 union workhouses that had been built by 1840 were in the south of England. It was in the north where resistance to the new Act was strongest and its implementation delayed. Few workhouses were built in Lancashire until the 1860s and Yorkshire's

A Glimpse of Workhouse Life in mid-nineteenth-century England

Charles Shaw was born in August 1832 at Tunstall in Staffordshire and after being educated at a dame school spent his childhood working, like his father and siblings, in the potteries. In later life, while running a cotton-spinning business, Shaw entered the ministry of the Methodist New Connexion Church. In 1903, three years before his death, he wrote *When I was a Child*, which was immortalised by Arnold Bennett in his novel *Clayhanger*. The story of Darius Clayhanger's childhood is directly based on Shaw's autobiography with its haunting description of poverty and life as a child worker. In 1842 Shaw's father lost his job after participating in a strike and the following extract from his book recounts the family's traumatic experience when they were forced by necessity into the Wolstanton and Burslem union workhouse at Chell.

Early in the morning we left a home without a morsel of food. We called on a relative who had kindly provided breakfast for us, and yet it was a wretched meal for my parents. I remember the choking sobs, though I did not understand them as I did afterwards. I remember too, how the food seemed to choke as much as the sobs, and the vain entreaties to 'eat a little more'. We went by the field road to Chell, so as to escape as much observation as possible. One child had to be carried as she was too young to walk. The morning was dull and cheerless. I had been through those fields in sunshine, and when the singing of the birds made the whole scene very pleasant. Now, when the silence was broken, it was only by deep agonising sobs. If we could have seen what was driving us so relentlessly up that hill to the workhouse ('Bastile' as it was bitterly called then), we should have seen two stern and terrible figures – Tyranny and Starvation. No other powers could have so relentlessly hounded us along. None of us wanted to go, but we must go, and so we came to our big home for the first time. The very vastness of it chilled us. Our reception was more chilling still. Everybody we saw and spoke to looked metallic, as if worked from within by hidden machinery. Their voices were metallic, and sounded harsh and imperative. The younger ones huddled more closely to their parents, as if from fear of these stern officials. Doors were unlocked by keys belonging to bunches, and the sound of keys and locks and bars, and doors banging, froze the blood within us. It was all so unusual and strange, and so unhomelike. We finally landed in a cellar, clean and bare, and as grim as I have since seen in prison cells. We were told that this was the place where we should have to be washed and put on our workhouse attire. Nobody asked us if we were tired, or if we had had breakfast. We might have committed some unnameable crime, or carried some dreaded infection. 'No softening gleam' fell upon us, from any quarter. We were a part of Malthus's 'superfluous population', and our existence only tended to increase the poverty from which we suffered. 'Benevolence' he said, 'in a being so short sighted as man, would lead to the grossest error, and soon transform the fair and cultivated soil of civilised society into a dreary scene of want and confusion'. We youngsters were roughly disrobed, roughly and coldly washed, and roughly attired in rough clothes, our under garments being all covered up by a rough linen pinafore. Then we parted amid bitter cries, the young ones being taken one way and the parents (separated too) taken as well to different regions in that merciful establishment which the statesmanship of England had provided for those who were driven there by its gross selfishness and unspeakable crassness.

Our bedroom was a long and narrow room, with beds in rows on each side of the room. Down the middle of the room was a long, narrow passage. The bed clothing was scant enough, and the beds hard enough for athletic discipline. At the end of the room, near the staircase, was a wide, shallow tub. There were boys there as cruel as neglect and badness could make them. They soon found out the timid ones, and would 'walk the midnight air' to frighten all they could by ghostly appearances. A poor lad, seeking the tub at night, would sometimes shriek through some brutal attempt to frighten him. Every new boy had to sing a song or tell a tale – the others wanted a taste of his quality – the first night, and pitied was that boy to be who could neither sing nor tell a tale. Misfortune brought boys there who shrank to the very narrow of their souls from the brutalities, obscenities and coarseness allowed. Other boys there were verily 'children of the devil'; yet these two sorts of boys were forced into association and community.

The first day's experience of the Bastile was like most others and the nights too. On the Sunday, I remember, we were taken to church and the clergy-man came to our 'dining room' but, like the schoolmaster, not to dine with us. He was to say 'grace before meat' in place of the schoolmaster as it was a sacred day. He also gave us a preliminary homily as long as the sermon he had given in church. We were told on that day and other Sundays, as I well remember, of the great mercies we enjoyed, of the good food provided, of the comfortable clothing we had, and how we were cared for by those about us. All this was said while before us on the table lay a small hunk of bread, a small plate with a small slice of thin, very thin cheese, and some jugs of water. The New poor law was wise enough, economically considered, but there could have been the economy without the brutality and harshness and humiliation pressed into the souls of old and young. Any system which makes young boys ashamed of their existence must be somewhat devilish in its evil ingenuity, and that was what Bastile 'discipline' did for me.

(Extracts reproduced from Charles Shaw's *When I was a Child* (1903))

COUNTY of BERKS.

John Walter, Esquire, Sheriff
of the County aforesaid.

WHEREAS

NOTICE has been given to me, by ten of His Majesty's Justices of the Peace, acting in and for the said County, that Information upon Oath has been laid before them, that divers serious Riots and Disturbances have lately taken place within this County, and that there is just cause to believe that further riots are intended; and the said Justices having called upon me to take such measures as the Law requires for the preservation of the peace of the said County,---Now I do hereby, by virtue of my Office, call upon all Knights, Gentlemen, Yeomen, Husbandmen, Labourers, Tradesmen, Servants, and Apprentices, and all other male persons above the age of fifteen years, and able to travel, to be in readiness to aid and assist me in the preservation of the King's peace within the said County, upon pain of imprisonment.

Hereof fail not at your Peril.

Berkshire Record Office D/EPG/01/4/69

County of Berkshire notice. Faced with the threat of mechanisation, farm labourers rebelled. Riots, led by the shadowy Captain Swing, started in Kent and spread throughout much of southern England when hayricks were burned, buildings razed and threshing machines destroyed. Notices, typical of the one seen here, were posted calling on 'all male persons above the age of fifteen . . . upon pain of imprisonment' to aid in the preservation of the peace. (Reproduced by permission of Berkshire Record Office Ref: D/EPG/01/4/69))

last union workhouse, at Todmorden, did not open until 1877.

The law had been put to the test in the north of England almost immediately after its enactment. Here, more than anywhere else in the country, there were pockets of resistance. In the industrial towns more people were overwhelmed by poverty than could be catered for by the new law and there seemed little humane alternative than to continue paying outdoor relief.

The Poor Law Commission met this challenge with the Labour Test Orders of 1842. These stated that where outdoor relief was given, it should be in return for parish work and then not only in the form of cash, but also food and fuel. Restrictions were further strengthened in 1844 when all forms of outdoor relief were prohibited, although specific 'urgent' exceptions were allowed. These included the events of sickness or accident and payments to widows with dependent legitimate children or to the family of a soldier. But Guardians continued to ignore the Orders when, given the level of poverty, they were difficult to enforce. A way of circumventing the restrictions was found when 'sickness' was often cited as the reason for continuing to

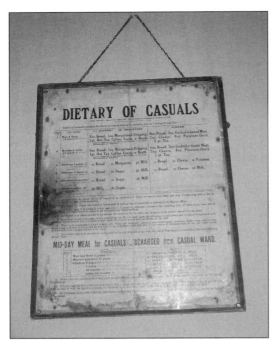

Workhouse 'casuals' – vagrants and tramps – were often accommodated in a separate ward. In return for a night's lodging they were expected to perform heavy manual work such as stone-breaking. Even as late as the twentieth century they were also entreated to a separate diet as suggested by this Public Assistance (Casual Poor) Order dated 1931, which was once displayed at Ripon workhouse. (Reproduced by permission of Simon Fowler)

pay outdoor relief to the able-bodied unemployed. It is estimated that sickness – real or alleged – was responsible for 75 per cent of all claims for outdoor poor-relief in the second half of the nineteenth century. In the face of mounting opposition the Poor Law Board (the successive organisation to the Poor Law Commission) was forced to retreat and in 1852 withdrew both the compulsory labour rule and the part payment of relief in kind.

In northern England there was also growing disquiet from those who were championing the Ten-Hour Movement – so called because its aim was to see legislation impose a maximum ten-hour working day – when the new Poor Law was seen as a further attack on the working population. In the factory towns of Lancashire and Yorkshire anti-Poor Law associations were formed and violent protests occurred in Bradford and Dewsbury before troops were dispatched to restore order. Throughout the country, with or without permission, Guardians continued to award outdoor relief. By 1850, when all but 12 per cent of the 1 million paupers being relieved in England and Wales were in receipt of outdoor relief, it was becoming clear that a lynch-pin of the new Poor Law was proving impossible to implement.[16]

Advocates of the new Poor Law argued that 'the principle of less eligibility', or 'the workhouse test', inevitably meant that it would be harsh for those who accepted indoor relief. And it was. Every aspect of life in the workhouse was governed by orders and regulations issued by the Poor Law Commission, either in the form of universally adopted 'General Orders' or 'Special Orders' intended for specific workhouses. These orders, applying to the management and operation of workhouses, culminated in 1847 in the issue of a 'Consolidated General Order', which was to become the long-established and frequently referred to manual of workhouse operation. Under the workhouse regime no concession was made for married couples;

Samford Poor Law Union

On 23 April 1848 Samuel, son of Jonathan and Ann Pinner of Bentley, was baptised in Tattingstone workhouse in Suffolk. Searching for the records of the child led to the discovery of the following account of the father's affairs in the Samford union minute books. A full account of how the Samford Poor Law union was run is explored in Sheila Hardy's *The House on the Hill: The Samford House of Industry, 1764–1930* (2001).

On 28 Aug 1851 at the weekly meeting of the Samford incorporation, with Mr Thomas Howard in the chair – Jonathan Pinner, labourer, was brought before J H L Anstruster Esq on a warrant charged with having left his wife and family chargeable to the parish of Bentley, the case having been heard by that gentleman and not withstanding the prisoner having several times been guilty of the same offence, and promised he would in future conduct himself properly, take his family from the house, maintain them and that he would not again give the officers any trouble if the parish would give him employment whereupon with the recommendation of the meeting the prisoner was discharged with the understanding of his taking his wife and family with him.

Further research here might include checking the overseers' records or constables' papers, gaol records and newspaper reports for reference to Jonathan's absconding.

Suffolk Record Office sources used: Samford union births, 1848–1946, ADA7/CB1; Samford union quarterly meeting minutes, 1850–1853, ADA7/AB1/10.

(Reproduced by permission of Historical Suffolk Research Service) families were divided by age and sex; inmates were depersonalised with the issue of pauper uniforms and deprived of personal possessions; and personal freedoms were curtailed or at best minimal.

Designed to increase the deterrent effect, the daily routine in the workhouse was monotonous and the work deliberately arduous and unpleasant. Oakum picking, the process of untwisting old ropes so that the fibres could be reused, was a common task for both men and women. Although later prohibited, the most infamous work was bone crushing, when the ground dust was sold as fertiliser to local farmers. Anti-Poor Law campaigners argued that inmates were routinely starved, but the amount of food recommended by the Poor Law Commission was often greater than that consumed in the outside community. Indeed, the principle of 'less eligibility' became difficult to maintain, given the depths of poverty that existed outside the workhouse. The model 'dietaries', contained in the General Orders issued by the Commission, were more nutritious and contained, for example, more meat than in meals consumed by the poorest labourers in their own home.

Despite the strict rules, or because of them, there were well-publicised incidents of abuse. Women and children were allegedly flogged by sadistic workhouse masters and, in the quest for 'less eligibility', paupers were starved. Much of the cruelty was localised and unofficial, as it was with a scandal at a workhouse in the Hampshire town of Andover. In March 1846, a Parliamentary Select Committee was appointed to investigate allegations of wrongdoing, and found that inmates had been systematically underfed and were forced to eat the marrow and the rotting flesh off the bones they were given to grind. The workhouse master was also shown to be a bully who inflicted cruel punishments and sexual abuse on those in his charge. The result of the parliamentary investigation, which found the workhouse master unfit to hold office, condemned the local Board of Guardians for inadequate supervision, and led ultimately in 1847 to the Poor Law Commission being dissolved and replaced by a Poor Law Board.

If the able-bodied found life in the workhouse hard, then so too did the sick. In earlier days most of the inmates had been able-bodied and under the age of 60. With a decline in able-bodied paupers being admitted to the workhouse, their numbers were increasingly replaced by the pauper sick. As the aged and infirm entered workhouses in greater numbers there was a corresponding increase in the need for

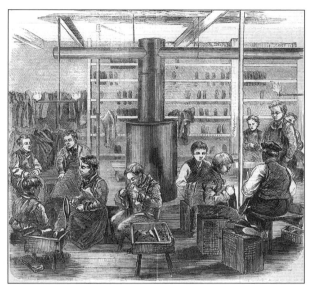

Training pauper children 'in the habits of industry' had long been one of the tenets of the Poor Laws. As early has 1563 there was a requirement that children of the poor, on reaching the age of 11 years, were to be taught a trade and set to work. But, by the nineteenth century, the conditions in which some children were taught were left wanting. According to a report written by James Kay, the Assistant Poor Law Commissioner, dated 1 May 1839, in some establishments 'efficient teachers had not been procured, proper books and apparatus were wanting; the arrangement of the routine and organisation of the school exhibited a complete ignorance of method, and universally the industrial instruction was meagre and purposeless'. (Illustrated London News)

medical care and nursing. Almost all workhouses had an infirmary ward for the care of the sick, with female inmates frequently undertaking nursing care, often in appalling conditions. The quality of care and the conditions endured by patients came to the attention of the medical journal *The Lancet*, which took up the cause and supported a campaign for reform. It announced the establishment of its own inquiry into the London workhouses to which it was able to obtain admission: 'Compare it with our public hospitals . . . workhouse hospitals sin by their construction, by their want of nursing, by their comfortless fittings, by the supremacy which is accorded to questions of expense, by the imperfect provision made for skilled medical attendants, and the wretched pittances to which they are ground down'.[17] A series of subsequent articles went on to summarise the results of their inquiry which appeared fortnightly in *The Lancet* over the next twelve months. They also included interviews with former workhouse staff. One of whom was Matilda Beeton, a former nurse at Rotherhithe:

> many sick patients were dirty, and that their bodies crawling with vermin; sheets were changed once in three weeks and soiled sheets had to be washed in the infirmary at night; there was a bad supply of towels used for every clean and dirty purpose; beds were made of flock and maggots would crawl from them by hundreds; the sick diet was a mockery – milk was not heard of.[18]

Conditions in the workhouse had also been the concern of other reformers including the daughter of the rector of All Saints' Church in Colchester. In 1853, after visiting the Strand Union workhouse to see a former colleague, Louisa Twining conceived the idea of arranging regular visits to workhouses by neighbourhood ladies (she believed middle-class women had a natural aptitude for helping the poor) to say prayers and converse with the inmates. Initially rejected by the Poor Law Board, which saw it as unwarranted interference, Twining went on to form the Workhouse Visiting Society which did much to encourage improvements in workhouse accommodation. Reform of workhouse infirmaries was one of Twining's prime concerns. The hardship and neglect suffered by the impoverished sick, confirmed by *The Lancet* in 1866, encouraged her to form the Association for Promoting Trained Nursing in Workhouse Infirmaries and Sick Asylums to train and supply nurses and secure the appointment of trained matrons. In 1885 she also joined and promoted Florence Nightingale's scheme to send trained nurses to the homes of the urban poor – a forerunner to the district-nurse movement.

It was campaigns such as those championed by *The Lancet*, Twining and Nightingale that led to the introduction of the Metropolitan Poor Act, which required the Poor Law authorities to establish the Metropolitan Asylums Board to care for London's sick poor. London's Poor Law unions and parishes combined into districts to raise contributions for a Common Poor Fund. This funded the building of separate hospitals for the poor, paid doctors' salaries, trained nursing staff and purchased drugs and medical equipment. The construction of three hospitals for the treatment of smallpox and fever soon followed the Act's introduction and these were established at Hampstead,

Homerton and Stockwell. For the insane, two hospitals were built at Leavesden and Caterham, both opening in autumn of 1870. In 1873 'imbecile' children were provided with a separate hospital, where for the first time teachers were engaged in an experiment to educate 'idiot' children. Available bed spaces for the sick poor were soon failing to keep pace with demand and further hospitals were built throughout London, notably at Deptford and Fulham, and at Greenwich, two redundant naval sailing ships, the *Atlas* and the *Endymion,* were also requisitioned.

To seize political control of Poor Law administration (and to be more responsive to public opinion) the Poor Law Board was established and managed by central government. But its membership, comprising Cabinet Ministers and other Members of Parliament, had inherited the legacy of the easement of outdoor-relief restrictions, which was becoming a cause for concern. The first remedial action came in 1865 when the cost of poor-relief was moved from individual parishes to the Poor Law unions. Now parishes contributed a poor rate, not based on its number of paupers, but instead assessed on its rateable value. Until then rural parishes, often with large numbers of paupers, paid the highest amount of money when they might be the poorest in the union. Despite this measure, overall spending on outdoor relief in the 1860s had increased by over 25 per cent, when Guardians saw it as the cheaper and, for the empathic, a more humane way to relieve poverty. The average cost of maintaining a pauper in the workhouse was 6s a week (equivalent to about £13 today), whereas that of outdoor relief was 2s (about £4 today).[19] When a typical labourer's weekly wage might be 11s (around £24 today), this small weekly allowance, calculated to be just enough to keep body and soul together, assumed a recipient's household income would be supplemented either by private charity or the result of pooling a family's wages.

Prior to 1839, **Ireland** had no Poor Law system of any kind, and with the increasing pressure of population the need for some such provision had become more and more obvious. In 1833, when the reform of the English Poor Law system was being considered, the government appointed a Commission under the chairmanship of Richard Whatley, Archbishop of Dublin, to inquire into the need for a system of poor-relief in Ireland. The commissioners instituted an investigation and concluded that the deterrent English system, the fundamental aim of which was to force the poor to find work, was totally unsuitable in

Ireland. Here there was a predominantly rural population and the root cause of Irish poverty was lack of employment. The Commission's proposals were hardly even considered, clashing as they did with government policy.

A new inquiry was entrusted to one of the English Poor Law Commissioners, George Nicholls, who conducted a hasty tour of the country in barely nine weeks and reported in favour of extending the English workhouse system to Ireland. His recommendation was accepted and an 'Act for the more Effectual Relief of the Destitute Poor in Ireland' was enacted in April 1838. The main provisions of the Act were as follows:

• The country was to be divided into 160 Poor Law unions;
• Each union was required to provide a workhouse for the relief of the destitute poor of that union;
• A compulsory rate was to be levied on the union to finance the administration of the Poor Law;
• A Board of Guardians was to be elected in each union to administer the Poor Law.

The system was originally designed to accommodate 1 per cent of the population, or 80,000 people, but by March 1851, famine had driven almost 4 per cent of the population into the workhouses. As the nineteenth century progressed the Poor Law unions were given many additional functions, particularly in relation to health, housing and sanitation.

Under the Local Government Act of 1898, Irish Poor Law unions lost some of their housing and sanitation functions to newly established rural district councils, but remained responsible for poor-relief. The early 1920s saw the abolition of Poor Law unions in the south of Ireland (with the exception of Dublin) and the closure of workhouses to reduce costs. Some workhouses were burned during 'the troubles' of the 1920s when the Irish republican movement fought for independence, while others were converted into country homes for the gentry or district hospitals.

Neither did the English Poor Law Amendment Act extend to Scotland but here, too, by the mid-nineteenth century reform was also called for. In 1843, the Church of Scotland, which had retained responsibility for poor-relief since 1597, was embroiled in the 'disruption' that led to almost half of its ministers deserting to establish

A Glimpse of Daily life in Scotland's Poorhouses

A report in the 'Dundee Year Book 1886–1890' gives us an insight into the background of those people who had no other choice than to apply for entry into the (Dundee) Combination Poorhouse known as the East Poorhouse. It depicts an awful scene. All those who wished to enter the poorhouse and those who didn't but circumstances left them no other choice had to go on their first visit to the Office of the Combination Parochial Board, which was situated at the Vault area of town. If you passed there any day of the week you could see the most wretched people congregating, waiting their turn to be seen: '. . . mothers, with children in their arms, and little dirty boys and girls hanging to their skirts; young men and women, pinched with hunger and weary worn by tramping about; and elderly persons of both sexes, hardly able to creep along the streets. All of them appear to have been beaten in the struggle for existence'.

These people could not just go up to the doors of the poorhouse and ask for entry. They had a rigorous process to go through before they could finally enter this establishment.

Following one of these applicants may give us in the twenty-first century a better idea of what life was like in the nineteenth century for ordinary people who fell on hard times through no fault of their own.

John was a 68-year-old man who had been married and had children. He was classed as a 'bit o' a lad' and was not one for sitting at home with his wife and children. He preferred to go out and 'meet the boys'. His wife died after twenty years of married life and this left John with a grown-up family who did not have any respect for their father. One by one they left home and John was left on his own to drink away his meagre earnings. As he got older he was troubled with rheumatic attacks which compelled him, in the end, to give up work. Within a few days he was reduced to a condition of starvation. He then tried to eke out his subsistence by selling small articles that he had made but this was not successful and after a further attack of rheumatics he had to apply for parochial relief.

Inquiries were instigated to find out about his character and his career to date and a report was laid before the Relief Committee. After deliberation the Committee offered John a place in the poorhouse and he accepted.

The next step on the road to the poorhouse is the probationer's stage. John is given a place in the probationers' ward where he is duly stripped of his filthy, tattered garments and given a bath. He then must go to bed and await the arrival of the doctor who will vouch for his state of health and say whether John is a genuine candidate for relief. John is believed to be a genuine candidate and is given a haircut and is sent to an ordinary ward for men. He will now pass his days in the poorhouse.

John is seen as one of the less troublesome inhabitants than for example a mother and her 'brood' of children. On many occasions those who ran the establishment were accused of cruelty in the handling of those who through no fault of their own had to seek refuge. In many cases these families would turn up at the poorhouse in an extremely filthy condition. Purifying these families could cause great distress but it was a task that was necessary when you consider that the institute could house at least 700 individuals. Therefore it was most important to have a regime which involved rigorous cleanliness on entry to the establishment.

There was a view that there were many people who could work for a living but that they believed the poorhouse would be a better bet. They would prefer to enter the poorhouse and subject themselves to its discipline, labour for eight hours a day and be fed and housed rather than do an honest days work for their own independence. Labour tests were instigated in the East Poorhouse in an effort to reduce the number of those with this lax moral outlook on life.

These candidates were put to work in sheds which were isolated from the other inhabitants. These sheds were about the size of a prison cell and were lighted from the roof and were heated by hot water pipes. Two of the sheds were equipped for stone-breaking and they only had a three quarters roofed area. These jobs were given to the worst class of inmate and convicts returning in to society. This is such a gruelling task that many of those put to it do not tarry long in the poorhouse.

The second test labour section was sack sewing and this was a far lighter mode of work but again a solitary occupation. After a week working at this it was noted how many sacks an individual has sewn and if that individual wishes to stay at the poorhouse s/he must sew the same amount of sacks or have their food ration cut. Most individuals did not stay long in the poorhouse once they had been put in the test sheds.

An example of this is Joe. Joe was a 57-year-old, unmarried man who had sold fish in the streets of Dundee for many years. He was known to have led a rather insecure life, fell on hard times, applied for relief and was offered the poorhouse. He accepted and by some mistake was sent to the West Poorhouse. This poorhouse was known to many as the 'House of Lords'. Joe will in time come to realise why it has been given this name.

He presents himself at the West Poorhouse with his ticket of admission and enters this establishment and lives 'in clover'. That is until a Visiting Committee of the Board spot Joe who is known to be 'a character' and they realise a mistake has been made. There is an inquiry and the result is that Joe must transfer to the East Poorhouse.

Joe is moved to the East Poorhouse and finds the change in conditions quite alarming. Instead of having a genteel life like that which he had in the West Poorhouse he is now separated from his companions and put to work in the test sheds under solitary conditions.

When asked about his experience of the different poorhouses Joe admits to having been quite happy in the West Poorhouse where he could pass the day chatting to his chums. What he disliked most about the East Poorhouse was being shut up in a solitary way. He was able to sew forty sacks a day and he never went over that amount.

(Reproduced by permission of Jessie Sword and the Friends of Dundee City Archives) the alternative Free Church of Scotland. With the Church of Scotland's ability to administer poor funds through its Kirk sessions severely diminished, a Commission of Inquiry was established to report and make recommendations for a revised system of poor-relief in Scotland.

When the Commission's Report was published in May 1844, it noted that poor-relief for the able-bodied was rare and concentrated its findings on establishing adequate means of support for the more deserving; the orphaned child, the infirmed and the frail aged poor. It recommended that each of Scotland's 880 parishes should be managed by a Central Board of Supervision with local parochial boards appointed to raise poor-relief funds either voluntarily or by imposing a compulsory parish poor rate 'according to the established usage'. It also recommended the appointment of local inspectors of the poor who, mirroring the duties of overseers in England and Wales, would examine all applications for poor relief.

The Commission's proposals were put into effect with the 'Amendment and better Administration of the Laws relating to the Relief of the Poor in Scotland Act' in August 1845. Unlike the requirements of the Poor Laws in England and Wales (and later extended to Ireland), relief was not confined to the workhouse. Instead the deserving poor were to receive outdoor relief and **parochial boards** were free to decide whether or not to provide a workhouse. If they were to be built then individual parishes could unite together to form 'Combinations' and operate a joint, shared establishment. The proposed system of collecting poor rates voluntarily was also endorsed by the Act. Although in time this was gradually superseded by a compulsory assessment on householders, in 1845, only 230 of Scotland's 880 parochial boards, managed by a Board of Supervision, were levying a compulsory tax, but by 1853 this had increased to 680.

Although the majority of Scotland's paupers received outdoor relief, over seventy workhouses were eventually built in Scotland, three-quarters of which were managed by 'Combinations'. The able-bodied were excluded but in the late nineteenth century workhouses, notably in urban areas, established separate wards to accommodate inmates who were considered unworthy of indoor relief. Housed in 'test wards', isolated from other inmates, these perceived 'vagrants and rogues' were fed basic rations and required to undertake heavy manual work to establish whether or not they were able to support themselves outside of the workhouse. In 1894, the Board of Supervision was

Week's Dietary for 150 Inmates – Huddersfield Workhouse, April 24th, 1848.

Day	Breakfast	Dinner	Supper
Sunday			
Monday			
Tuesday			
Wednesday			
Thursday			
Friday			
Saturday			

Example of a workhouse diet from Huddersfield, 1848. The workhouse diet was often more nutritional than that on which many others survived. Many lower income families survived on a diet often restricted to bread, cheese, vegetables and adulterated tea used over and over again. A labourer's daily food typically consisted of a breakfast of hot water poured over bread and flavoured with onion. This was followed by a dinner of bread and cheese, eaten in the fields or workplace, washed down with ale or cider and a supper of potatoes or cabbage greased with bacon fat. (Reproduced by permission of The National Archives (Ref MH12/15070))

replaced by a Local Government Board and in turn parish councils assumed the duties of parochial boards.

In England and Wales, the equivalent of the Board of supervision, the Poor Law Board, had been replaced by a centrally controlled Local Government Board in 1871. This had a wider brief, not only for the operation of the Poor Laws, but also for the equally sensitive nineteenth-century social problems of health and welfare. With hardship and poverty increasingly being eased by handouts from private charities – the Board actively encouraged Poor Law unions to work in tandem with large charitable bodies, such as the **Charity Organisation Society** – the new organisation took decisive action to curtail spending and lessen the burden on ratepayers of paying for outdoor relief: 'the increase in the cost of outdoor relief is so great, as to excite apprehension; and to suggest that measures should be taken, not only to check any further increase, but to diminish the present amount . . .', wrote the author of a circular issued to all Guardians.[20] In

Labour in the Workhouse

Manual labour was seen as an essential ingredient of workhouse life. This included oakum picking – the process of untwisting old ropes so the fibres could be reused. It was a task also given to prisoners to peform. In his book *Criminal Prisons in London and Scenes of Prison Life* (1862), Henry Mayhew describes the process: 'prisoners were given a weighed quantity of old rope cut into lengths equal to that of a hoop stick. Some of the pieces are white and sodden looking, others are hard and black with tar upon them. The prisoner takes up a length of junk and untwists it and when he has separated it into so many corkscrew strands, he further unrolls them by sliding them backwards and forwards on his knee with the palm of his hand until the meshes are loosened. The strand is further unravelled by placing it in the bends of a hook fastened to the knees and sawing it smartly to and fro which soon removes the tar and grates the fibres apart. In this condition, all that remains to be done is loosen the hemp by pulling it out like cotton wool, when the process is completed . . . The place is full of dust . . . the shoulders of the men are covered with brown dust almost as thick as the shirt front of a snuff taker . . . the hard rope cuts and blisters their fingers'. Oakum picking was unpleasant and workhouse inmates and prisoners alike were punished if their work failed to meet expectations. Sometimes they were paid, hence the phrase 'money for old rope'.

Men picking oakum. (Reproduced by permission of Simon Fowler)

reminding his readers of the need for financial prudence, the writer goes on to note the contemporary view that recipients had become unnecessarily dependent on outdoor relief: 'A certainty of obtaining out-door relief in his own home whenever he may ask for it extinguishes in the mind of the labourer all motive for husbanding his resources, and induces him to rely exclusively upon the [poor] rates instead of upon his savings for such relief as he may require'.

The other area ripe for attention was the workhouse. Already viewed with fear and hatred, life for the poor in these 'Bastilles', as they came to be called, was to become even harsher. In 1871, the Local Government Board initiated an experiment whereby only able-bodied paupers would be admitted to a workhouse and there set to work on hard manual labour in return for a subsistence allowance for their families. With separate arrangements being made for the existing sick and the elderly, the first workhouse to be included in the trial was at Poplar in East London. Such were the levels of hardship imposed that it soon proved to be a strong deterrent and the scheme was extended to provincial city workhouses, notably in the Midlands and the north west. However, it came to be seen by Guardians as a 'quick-fix' solution to rid themselves of their more troublesome, more expensive and less desirable paupers. In 1880, two years before it reverted to its original purpose, Poplar's Medical Officer noted with dismay that the majority of inmates were not able-bodied and a quarter of those admitted were over the age of 60.

The crackdown on outdoor relief and a more aggressive stance on workhouse admissions, together with the benevolence of private charities, helped bring about the desired effect. Between 1870 and the end of the century, although the number of workhouse paupers increased from 156,000 to 254,644, those benefiting from outdoor relief fell from 876,000 to 387,208. This was partly due to a more rigorous campaign in the administration of relief, and partly as a result of an overall growth in the industrial economy. When measured against the total population, the proportion of paupers declined from 5.7 per cent to 2.5 per cent. During the first decade of the twentieth century the percentage of paupers continued to fall, but the figures only served to mask the true extent and nature of poverty. As the historian Edward Royle notes, 'The [new] Poor Law did not relieve the main body of poverty in nineteenth century Britain; it merely provided a harsh and undesirable safety-net for the absolutely destitute'.[21]

Chapter 6

CHARITY AND SELF-HELP IN THE INDUSTRIAL AGE

'They live their lives before each others' eyes and their joys and
sorrows are the common property of the entire community'
George Sims, *How the Poor Live, and Horrible London*, 1899

B y the start of the nineteenth century the industrial and economic
transformation of Britain was well under way. Radical changes to
working practices, overcrowded industrial towns, dislocation
caused by the Napoleonic Wars and agricultural mechanisation,
together with a rapid increase in the population, all conspired to create
increased levels of poverty and social distress. There was an urgent
need for effective relief. The revolution in industry was the catalyst that
led to amendments in the 'old' Poor Laws, but in 1800 private charity
was more important in the day-to-day relief of poverty. A plethora of
charities were in existence; small amounts of money were disbursed to
needy families in the form of parochial assistance; almshouses
provided accommodation, albeit for a relative few; children of the poor
were receiving a modest education; and the sickly poor were being
treated in subscription or 'voluntary' hospitals. But by then they were
far from meeting contemporary needs. Many, charities with
geographically restricted roles, established when Britain was
predominantly an agricultural nation, had become obsolete when
those who once depended on them moved away to find work in the
new industrial towns.

There was mounting concern too that funds were being fettered
away on some ancient or forgotten provision and of trustees being
incompetent or simply corrupt. Sufficient suspicion of fund misuse had
existed for a number of local investigations to take place by
commissioners appointed under the 1601 Charities Act. As early as the
seventeenth century, the churchwardens of a Nottinghamshire parish

were called to account when rent, intended to help the poor, had found its way into the pockets of local landowners. The situation had improved little a century later when a committee, formed to investigate charitable misuse in Ipswich, reported, 'It is reasonable to expect that the original design of the donors of publick charities, should, in process of time, be forgotten or mistaken; from hence the mismanagement and misapplication of them must arise'.[1]

Many endowments and **trust deeds**, particularly those for hospitals and almshouses dating from the medieval period, with funds derived from landownership had also significantly out grown the purpose of their original bequest. Here too individuals benefited at the expense of those it was intended to help. At Christ's Hospital in Sherburn, County Durham, for example, where by 1830 the annual rental income had grown to a healthy £2,500. Trustees, having paid for the upkeep of the building and sustenance for its almshouse residents, awarded the master the residual £1,100 as a salary.

Almsmen – known as in-brethren – and nursing staff at Sherburn Hospital, County Durham, photographed between 1914 and 1934. During this period the Revd Douglas Samuel Boutflower (standing second from the right) was master. The lady in black crinoline was presumably Mrs Boutflower. Inmates could often be seen in Durham wearing their distinctively cut brown suits. (Reproduced by permission of the Trustees of Sherburn House Charity)

The result of concerns – that charitable donations 'appear to have been lost, and others from the neglect of payment and the inattention of those persons who ought to superintend them'[2] – resulted in the introduction of the Act 'For the registering and securing of Charitable Donations' in 1812. More commonly known by its sponsoring Member of Parliament, (Sir Samuel) Romilly, it sought to require magistrates to compile registers of charitable endowments, but was not a great success. With insufficient enforcement provision, by 1829 only 696 charities had registered. The next stage in bringing about effective charity control involved a Scottish advocate whose actions were to sow the seeds of the present day **Charity Commission**.

In 1816, Henry Brougham, Member of Parliament and vice-president of the newly formed British and Foreign School Society, successively pressed Parliament for an investigation into charitable endowments. This started with a Select Committee 'to inquire into the education of the lower orders in the Metropolis'.[3] By 1820, Brougham had established a board of twenty commissioners and was able to extend the remit 'to examine all trusts, report and certify their findings and to make suggestions for the avoidance of any future misapplication of funds'. Not only did this include educational charities, but all 29,000 other endowed charities then known to exist in England, Wales and Scotland. To achieve these aims the commissioners were given the authority to call witnesses, administer oaths and to demand documents. In the nineteenth century to undertake investigations of this nature and publish reports making recommendations for change was an innovative venture and was the first of the type of government-initiated inquiry we often see in operation today. The commissioners reported almost continuously from 1816 until 1853, when their work was superseded by the appointment of a permanent Charity Commission.

In 1909 the Royal Commission on the Poor Laws (see Chapter 7) estimated the total income of private charities was £1 million, of which two-thirds went on specific needs (for example, medical facilities and accommodating the elderly) and one-third spent on the poor generally. Thousands of endowed charities and trust funds disbursed sums of money to the poor of their own communities. But even these were overshadowed by the extent of voluntary or **subscription charities** providing succour to the poor. Throughout the country they ranged from national bodies such as the Church of England Waifs and Strays Society to local enterprises when, for example, the Liverpool Food

Association (later known as the Food and Betterment Association and today as the League of Welldoers) collected money to provide meals at 1/2*d* to the poor (and free to the poorest) in its home town. But it was in London where the sums were most impressive. According to the publisher and philanthropist Sampson Low in his book *Charities of London*, published in 1862, there were 640 institutions, ranging from 124 colleges, hospitals, almshouses and other asylums for the aged, 80 medical hospitals and infirmaries, 72 professional and trade provident and benevolent funds, 56 Bible and missionary societies, 16 charities for the blind, deaf, dumb and crippled, 14 asylums for orphaned children, and 4 Indian famine funds. Their collective annual income from property investment was £841,373 and a further £1,600,594 in voluntary contributions.[4] The importance placed on organised charitable relief is evident when these sums are compared with the estimated £1.4 million spent each year in Greater London alone by the Metropolitan Poor Law authorities.

Medical treatment for the poor also attracted charitable donations. Until the advent of the voluntary subscription hospital medical facilities were completely unorganised and the only institutions in the country available to the poor were London's five royal chartered hospitals (see Chapter 4). The wealthy sought the services of a physician or surgeon and operations were preformed in their own homes, but for the poor this was not possible. A report of 1690 suggested that 'The usual Fee of a Doctor in ancient times was 20*s* and that had not taken a Degree, 10*s*. But now there is no certain Rule, but some that are Eminent have received in Fees Yearly of 2000 or 3000£'.[5] When the report was written approximately one-fifth of the total population was earning something less than £7 a year.

London's Westminster Infirmary was the first of a new form of charity – the voluntary hospital. Established in 1719, it owed its existence to the charitable aims of the Westminster Society which acknowledged that great numbers of the sick were not entitled to parochial relief. Voluntary hospitals differed from the existing chartered institutions in several important aspects. They were dependent on voluntary subscriptions or contributions rather than on endowments for financial support; medical and surgical staff held honorary positions; and patients were not required to pay fees. In the provinces the first voluntary hospital was founded in 1736 at Winchester. And three years later Thomas Guy, a successful bookseller who had accumulated a vast fortune from shrewd overseas

The Shadwell Hospital for Women and Children

Appalled by the effects of cholera outbreaks in 1866, Dr Nathaniel Heckford and his wife Sarah converted a disused warehouse to create the East London Hospital for Children and Dispensary for Women. Such were the tireless efforts of the doctor that he died within five years of its opening at the young age of 29. The hospital, funded entirely by donations, had the backing of Charles Dickens, whose articles about the hospital garnered powerful supporters.

In 1877 the hospital moved into new premises and the Duchess of Tech, granddaughter of George III, conducted the opening ceremony. The royal family continued its support with Princess Marie Louisa being a regular visitor and campaigner. In 1942 the hospital became part of the Queen Elizabeth Hospital for Children, before closing in April 1963.

investments, founded Guy's Hospital. It was Guy's generosity that provided the momentum for a growth in the voluntary hospital movement. In 1721, Alexander Munro, a teacher of anatomy, wrote a pamphlet advocating the need for a hospital and raised £2,000 in subscriptions for Scotland's first medical establishment for the poor. There are many hospitals in existence today that carry the name of an early benefactor, amongst these are John Radcliffe in Oxford and John Addenbrooke in Cambridge. By 1861 there were 23 teaching hospitals and 130 voluntary general hospitals in England and Wales funded by philanthropic subscriptions. Within these establishments nearly 12,000 beds were available for the 'deserving poor' who, in urbanised areas debilitated by poor diets and inadequate housing, were the most susceptible to illness and disease. While subscribers continued to be the mainstay of hospital funding, further support was gained from the Hospital Saturday Fund, introduced in the 1850s to collect weekly contributions from workers' pay which continued well into the twentieth century.

Patients seeking hospitalisation were first required to obtain the recommendation of a hospital subscriber that their admittance was 'a proper object of the charity' and pay a deposit towards the cost of burial should they die while under hospital care. At the Leicester Infirmary – which until 1773 required a 12s deposit – patients were required to obtain a letter from the Overseer of the Poor confirming that the cost of removing their body, and the funeral expenses, would be met by the parish. Paying this 'caution-money' encouraged the

Penny in the Pound Fund

In 1871 the Liverpool Voluntary Hospitals Council set up the 'Penny in the Pound Fund'. In return for contributing one penny in every pound they earned, members were entitled to receive free in-patient care in the city's voluntary hospitals. The fund's origin lay in the Hospital Saturday and Sunday Funds, which helped ensure the city's voluntary hospitals received a regular income that guaranteed medical treatment to members. The Saturday Fund collection took place on payday, and the Sunday Fund was boosted by Church collections. In 1927 the two funds were merged and become the Merseyside Hospitals Council.

After the Second World War, the Council offered a convalescence home to its members at 'Brockhole', situated on the shores of Lake Windermere in, what was then, Westmorland. With the introduction of the Health Service in 1948, responsibility for the city's voluntary hospitals passed to the NHS, and the Penny in the Pound Fund was remodelled to offer convalescence and cash grants to members and dependants. Its name was changed to Medicash in 1984, and the fund continues to provide members with a range of services, including amenities within NHS hospitals and residential homes.

belief that hospitals were a gateway to death – a view no doubt supported by high surgical mortality rates and the practice of admitting patients with infectious diseases, like cholera, to general wards.

Complementing the work of **voluntary hospitals** were the dispensaries that offered the working classes and the poor an alternative, sometimes only, means of obtaining medical treatment. In the nineteenth century dispensaries were popular in Britain's industrial towns where voluntary hospitals failed to keep pace with the health demands associated with the rapid growth of the urban population. The first dispensary in Liverpool opened in 1781. Here, three physicians, three surgeons and an apothecary attended six days a week to meet the medical needs of the poor. In its annual report for 1820 the dispensary recorded having seen 14,000 patients who presented with ailments typical of the age, including typhus and pulmonary consumption. Provident dispensaries were also established where the low paid contributed a weekly sum towards the cost of treatment.

Giving to charity became a symbol of Victorian respectability. In one survey of middle-class households published in 1896 families spent more on charity than they did on any other item except food. They gave to an array of good causes, including the Metropolitan Visiting and Relief Association, which collected over £20,000 a year, and nationally to Queen Alexandra's appeal for the relief of distress, which by 1905 had raised £750,000. There were also non-institutional donations, ranging from a few pennies found in 'poor boxes' to the £81,838 collected by a nation willing to share the financial hardship endured by bereaving families after a mining disaster in 1862. William Howe, who regularly surveyed London charities in the second half of the nineteenth century, estimated the income of 800 of the 1,000 charities then known to operate in the city had risen to £3.1 million by 1894.[6] By way of comparison, the national expenditure of the Poor Law authorities in the same year was £9.2 million. It was a comparison that attracted the attention of *The Times* in 1895, when it claimed receipts from London charities exceeded the budget of several European governments.

In 1869, with such sums at stake there was a move to organise London's charitable endeavours when the 'Society for Organising Charitable Relief and Repressing Mendicity' was formed, more commonly known as the Charity Organisation Society (COS). Its aim was to organise existing charities and establish the worthiness of those seeking help to ensure private charity was not wasted or duplicated. The Society's philosophy was the belief that giving indiscriminately to the poor only served to encourage them to become reliant on charity rather than 'respectable' and independent citizens. The poor, it maintained, should be taught to help themselves through all the usual crises of life and assistance should only be given in dire, exceptional circumstances. This was achieved by investigation when COS volunteers conducted a close examination (what we would call 'means testing' today) into the lifestyles of claimants to establish whether or not the case was worthy of charitable assistance.

The COS, having spread beyond the metropolis, was a powerful organisation in the closing decades of the nineteenth century, but its success was not greeted with universal approval. Known to its critics as 'Cringe or Starve', due to its rigorous attitude to applicants for charitable support, charities were reluctant to surrender the right to decide how their money was spent. Those run on evangelical lines opposed the lack of compassion inherent in a process that all too strictly weeded out 'scroungers' and examined the needy. Because of this much of charity continued to be disbursed in an indiscriminate

Objectives of the Charity Organisation Society

The Society for Organising Charitable Relief and Repressing Mendicity was founded in 1869. It was much more commonly known by its short title of the Charity Organisation Society, or simply as the COS. Its objectives, as defined in the eighth annual report published in 1877, were:

1 To bring into harmonious co-operation with each other and with the Poor-Law authorities the various charitable agencies and individuals in the district, and thus effectually to check the evils of 'overlapping' relief caused by simultaneous but independent action.

2 To investigate thoroughly the cases of all applicants for charitable relief, whether they are referred to the offices for inquiry and report, or whether they apply of their own accord.

3 To place gratuitously at the disposal of all charitable agencies and private persons the investigating machinery of the Committees of the Society, and to send to persons having a legitimate interest in cases full reports of the results of the investigations made.

4 To obtain from the proper charities, or from charitable individuals, suitable and adequate relief for deserving cases.

5 To assist from its own funds, and as far as possible in the form of loans, all suitable cases for which adequate assistance cannot be obtained from other sources.

6 To repress mendicity by the above means, by the gratuitous distribution of Investigation Tickets, and by the prosecution of impostors.

7 To afford to the public at large information regarding the objects and mode of working of existing charities.

8 To promote, as far as possible, the general welfare of the poor, by means of social and sanitary reforms, and by the inculcation of habits of providence and self-dependence.

way. Despite the doubts and opposition, the pioneering work of the COS laid the foundation of modern social work. Its emphasis on individual causes of poverty and family case work continued into the twentieth century when in 1946 it became known as the **Family Welfare Association**.

The idea that people should help themselves rather than rely on the charity of others was also encouraged by the repressive nature of the

Huddled together. The author was unable to find any further information to explain this evocative image of a destitute mother and child – a picture is worth a thousand words. (Reproduced by permission of Simon Fowler)

Poor Law Amendment Act that threatened confinement in the workhouse for those who failed, or were unable, to make arrangements to deal with their poverty. It was as a result of the stigma associated with the workhouse regime that **friendly societies** came to prominence in the nineteenth century by performing a crucial role in the financial wellbeing of Britain's working classes. It has been estimated that by 1891 4 million working males, almost half the working population, were members of friendly societies, relying on them for insurance against sickness, pension provision, access to a doctor or funeral expenses. Trade unions (many of which have their roots in the friendly society movement) and co-operative societies were also formed to provide mutual aid. It was the friendly societies, however, that were by far the largest group and could boast, by the start of the twentieth century, that collectively they had nearly 10 million members in 18,000 societies, representing almost every village, town or trade.

Friendly societies were established either in small local communities with membership of a few dozen, or at a national level with many thousands of members. At their very simplest they were sick clubs where members paid an agreed weekly contribution. Some were dependent upon financial or social patronage; others fiercely independent and managed entirely by their own membership, but they all shared a common purpose of fraternity and mutuality. This engendered a sense of friendship and responsibility for each other's health and welfare and made occasions for celebration and festivities; a legacy of the parish guilds that once gathered on a patron's feast day to offer mass and distribute alms.

At the end of the eighteenth century the government, recognising that membership of friendly societies reduced the burden of Poor Law relief, did much to encourage their growth. The Friendly Societies Act

Wrington Friendly Society

The village of Wrington, 6 miles north-east of Axminister, had two friendly societies. In 1797, Hannah More, a local philanthropist and playwright who, with her sister Martha, also started Sunday schools in the locality, established the Wrington Female Friendly Society 'to secure by means of small quarterly payments, medical and pecuniary assistance to married women in case of childbirth; and in the event of the death of a member [where] a small contribution is levied from the whole of the members towards funeral expenses'.[7] Some twenty-five years later a Men's Friendly Society was founded for the benefit of agricultural labourers resident in the village.

In 1861 the female society – which held its anniversary on the last Tuesday in each June – had a service in the parish church, followed by tea in the National School Room. It had a fund of £525, to which its sixty-two members contributed £30 per year. The society was not dissolved until 1948 when the healthy sum of £938 was distributed amongst its forty-eight members.

The men's society received its certification from the Registrar of Friendly Societies in July 1852, after its trustees, including the Revd John Vane and surgeon Horace Swete, submitted a set of rules for approval. In addition to sickness benefit, the society made provision for two further benefits: if a member broke a bone, but not if it was the result of 'drunkenness, fighting or wrestling', and in the event of death, when each member paid to the widow or children the sum of 1s. If a member voluntarily joined the Army, Navy or Militia, his contributions stayed with the society when, upon his return, he would only pay one quarter of the arrears. The anniversary celebrations were held at the Golden Lion Inn each Trinity Wednesday, preceded by a church service, and a procession through the village with 'coloured ribbons and the staff, or pole, bearing the emblem of the society'. The society existed for another sixty years, before it was dissolved in 1920.

of 1793 required societies to submit rules to magistrates for approval, but in return gained certain privileges. Members, for example, were exempted from the law of settlement that allowed overseers to turn away anyone entering a parish seeking work who might claim poor-relief. It has been estimated that payments to members from friendly society funds was saving £2 million a year of Poor Law expenditure. Sir Frederick Morton Eden, an insurance company manager and writer on the state of the poor, reported in 1799, 'I do not find that any parish has been burdened with the maintenance of a member of any friendly society; nor instances of the families becoming burthensome'.

At the start of the nineteenth century there was a major shift in the friendly society movement when societies began operating as collective organisations. These new societies, or 'orders', offered, in the spirit of the age, a greater degree of democracy than the autocratic nature of many earlier societies. While branches maintained local autonomy by continuing to collect subscriptions and pay members who were unable to work due to illness, affiliation enabled them to share the more expensive payments when members died. With claims

Keevil Friendly Society

At the end of the eighteenth century, one of the early agricultural societies, the Bath and West of England Society, resolved to establish a friendly society in the Wiltshire village of Keevil.

Like all friendly societies, Keevil's membership of agricultural labourers had to pay contributions for a specified length of time. In this case, it was one year before they were 'free' to benefit from payments in times of illness from work. No payment was made to a member if his actions resulted in the illness where the rule stated: 'No person shall receive any Benefits from the Society in consequence of any disability or calamity originally proceeding from the following causes vis. Drunkenness, Venereal Disease, Cudgel Playing, Wrestling or Gambling Exercise'. Otherwise 6s was paid as 'bed' pay if they were confined by their illness, or a lesser amount as 'walking' pay. Unusually for Keevil's members, sickness benefits were also withdrawn if they contracted smallpox, but an allowance of £3 was paid for their burial if they were to die of the disease!

Keevil held its friendly society feast day on Whit Monday each year, when all members were expected to assemble at its headquarters at the Rose and Crown Inn, dressed in a black hat and coat, at 10.00 am for a procession around the parish bounds. In Wiltshire and Dorset, it was customary to wear ribbons tied around the hat in the colours of the Keevil village, which were red and blue.

of ancient and remote origins, they developed elaborate rituals and, like the Freemasons, had initiation ceremonies for new members, secret passwords and regalia such as banners, certificates, sashes and emblems.

It was in north-west of England, the heartland of the Industrial Revolution and where working conditions were particularly harsh, that these affiliated orders first began to appear. The Independent Order of Oddfellows – said to have originated from the 'odd fellows' who were not able to join any other medieval trade guild – started in Manchester in 1813. This expanded in the nineteenth century to become, with a membership of 4 million in 1874, the largest and most influential within the friendly society movement. The Ancient Order of Foresters, formed in 1834 from 100 separate guilds, had by 1914, 1.5 million members with funds in excess of £10 million. On Christmas Day 1826, twelve men met in Ashton-under-Lyne to establish the Loyal Order of Ancient Shepherds, and seven years later the United Ancient Order of Druids was formed, after disaffected members of an earlier order 'regrouped'. In a name reminiscent of an ancient trade guild, the National United Order of Free Gardeners was founded in Oldham in 1840 – although none were larger than either the Oddfellows or the Foresters.

Ancient Order of Foresters' Court record. A regular item of Ancient Order of Foresters' business, like all friendly societies, was a report on members who were 'on the funds'. The sickness lists are of particular interest in revealing details about an individual. The example seen here relates to a meeting of the Foresters' Court 'Egerton and Wyndham', Number 3260, held at Rustington, Sussex, on Monday 13 June 1881. (Reproduced by permission of Roger Logan)

Friendly society members paid a weekly contribution of 5*d* or 6*d* in return for 8*s* to 10*s* sickness benefit, payment of doctor's fees and a funeral grant of £10. For many, however, the weekly contribution was too much. For these, burial societies were a cheaper alternative. The shame of a pauper funeral lay behind the growth of **burial clubs**. If the poor had nothing else they at least wanted the dignity of a proper funeral when they died. Like the early friendly societies, theses groups were small local affairs. The Blackburn Philanthropic Burial Society, for example, provided a funeral grant of £5 in return for a weekly payment of 1*d*.

Membership of friendly societies was inevitably limited to better paid workers and the poorest were actively excluded. Workers in low-paid jobs generally found it impossible to pay the necessary contribution to qualify for sickness benefit. To a family living on £1 a week, every penny counted in the struggle for survival and even 6*d* was more than they could afford. The poorest also suffered (and indeed were poor) from irregularity of employment, such as agricultural seasonal work, when it was not possible to keep up the necessary

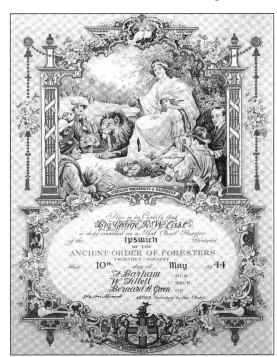

An Ancient Order of Foresters' membership certificate which records that George R W East was enrolled as a Chief Ranger in the Ipswich District of the Ancient order of Foresters. Officials within the friendly society movement were issued with elaborate membership certificates. (Reproduced by permission of Roger Logan)

regular payments that guaranteed protection against sickness.

The **co-operative movement** was another example of working class self-help. Co-operative shops, first introduced by the Rochdale Pioneers Society in 1844, were owned by their members, who received surplus profits in the form of a dividend, or as it became known, 'the divi'. By 1891 there were a million shareholders and the 'Co-op' had extended its activities to include friendly society type schemes such as life assurance and funeral provision. However, retail co-operatives had strict rules about not allowing credit when for the seasonally underemployed or the low wage earner 'buy now pay later' was an all too often survival strategy.

When the poorest were bypassed by organisational relief they turned to support of a more informal kind – that of family, friends and neighbours who could be relied on to rally round in times of sickness and need. In the overcrowded Victorian slums of industrial Britain there was a great deal of mutual welfare in the absence of help from institutions. In the midst of the acute and shared poverty there was empathy and a ready willingness to help neighbours in particular need. This support and generosity is illustrated in the oral testimony of one woman born in the London Borough of Hackney in 1903:

> And mother used to say to me 'poor Mrs Somebody next door. She's got no food in the house'. So mother used to have a good old nourishing stew, and she used to cook it in a big saucepan with handles on both sides. And I was the one to take it in to Mrs Somebody next door. And she'd say 'Oh, thank you ever so much!' and she used to feed the kids.[8]

The presence of large numbers of migrants from the same area served to strengthen the network of support. Irish neighbours, in the Summer Lane district of Birmingham, contributed money for funeral expenses if the dead person's kin could not raise enough. They loaned money and kitchen utensils, helped orphans to find jobs and lodgings, attended wakes and weddings. Newcomers were given a corner of a room in which to sleep and were helped in their search for work.

Mutual help also extended to childcare facilities when families fed each others' children, loaned food or circulated outgrown items of clothing around the community. The sick and the elderly would be cared for rather than see them consigned to the workhouse. Despite intolerable levels of overcrowding, the newly arrived would be found somewhere to stay. In his 1889 book, *How the Poor Live and Horrible*

London, the journalist George Sims noted these acts of charity, even at the cost of great hardship to the giver, were more common in poorer neighbourhoods.

> The poor are kinder to each other than the rich; they are bound by stronger ties of sympathy; their hearts respond more readily to generous impulses. They have greater opportunities of helping each other, and there are no barriers of pride between them. They live their lives before each others' eyes and their joys and sorrows are the common property of the entire community.[9]

Mutual aid, whether in the form of friendly society membership, shopping at the 'co-op' or selfless acts of generosity within poorer communities, was no substitute for a properly constructed welfare system, but it was, in many cases, the primary means by which the poorer Victorian working class survived.

In the twentieth century the voluntary charity sector found itself adapting to a changing political and social climate. A new Liberal government was pursing its own programme to combat poverty. As a result, charities and the state found their roles reversed. Instead of being a primary source to the poor, charities began to take on a supporting role to the state. It was a position too that charities were forced to adopt when donations, once expected from a working population, went instead on direct taxation and national-insurance contributions to pay for the statutory social-welfare measures. Throughout the inter-war years charities found themselves increasingly relying on appeals rather than regular donations and subscriptions.

In 1820, Henry Brougham oversaw the investigation of 29,000 charities with a total estimated income of £4.2 million. In March 2007 there were over 208,000 registered charities (20 per cent of which are for the prevention or relief of poverty) operating in the United Kingdom with a combined annual income in excess of £50 billion. And the sector continues to grow with an average of 5,000 new charities registering each year. It was surely with a degree of foresight that Lord Nathan reported in 1952: 'so far from voluntary action being dried up by the extension of the social services greater and greater demands are being made on it. We believe, indeed, that the democratic state, as we know it, could hardly function effectively without such channels for, and demands upon the voluntary (charity) sector'.[10]

Chapter 7

THE WELFARE STATE

'it relieved a mass of poverty and destitution which is too proud to
wear the badge of pauperism'
David Lloyd George, 1911

The work of Booth and Rowntree had shown that unemployment
was a cause of poverty amongst a 'residuum' of casual and
marginal workers, but by the end of the nineteenth century there
was mounting concern that even skilled workers were being plunged
into poverty due to lack of work. The economic boom years of the early
1870s had been succeeded by an extended period of trade depressions
that so alarmed the Victorians that they appointed a Royal
Commission on what they called the Great Depression in Trade and
Industry. They had assumed steady industrial growth would
guarantee an increasing demand for labour but the economic health of
the nation, allied to a rise in foreign competition, forced a reappraisal.
It became evident that periodic spells of mass unemployment even
amongst 'respectable' workers were the inevitable consequence as
patterns of trade and industry went through cycles of boom to bust.
The Poor Law was not designed to deal with a crisis of this kind.
Unemployment was not the result of any failing on the part of an
individual and furthermore, the workhouse system would simply not
have coped with the numbers involved.

After a protest meeting in 1886 of 20,000 unemployed workers at
Trafalgar Square developed into a riot, the government responded by
encouraging the Poor Law authorities to set up temporary work
schemes. In a circular to Boards of Guardians the Local Government
Board recommended they provide community work projects for the
unemployed, such as street cleaning, rather than admitting them to the
workhouse as subjects for pauper relief. At the start of the
twentieth century, as the number of unemployed increased, 400 men in
Leicester finally lost patience with the empty promises of work, or the

cold comfort of charity, and marched to London to bring attention to their plight.[1] This crusade, like many other protests that took place throughout the country, hastened the first legislative measure to alleviate the suffering of the 'respectable' unemployed and their families – the Unemployed Workmen Act of 1905. Towns were now expected to form local District Committees to establish relief work schemes to help the unemployed find jobs. Many of today's civic gardens and recreational grounds were first laid out as a result of work created under this Edwardian Act. This in turn led to the first labour exchanges opening up, and these had responsibility for ensuring that the unemployed knew where and when work was available.

In 1904 the growth in unemployment, together with increasing concerns about the suitability of the Poor Law to deal with the effects of poverty, led to the establishment of a Royal Commission on the Poor Laws. Under the chairmanship of Lord George Hamilton, its members comprised civil servants from the Local Government Board, Poor Law Guardians, members of the Charity Organisation Society, trade unionists, members of the clergy and the social investigators Charles Booth and Beatrice Webb (a cousin of Charles Booth's wife). The committee took four years to reach its conclusions and, in having undertaken hundreds of interviews and visits, was the most extensive investigation of the Poor Laws since the work of Nassau, Chadwick and others in 1834. But the commissioners failed to reach an agreement on how the system should be reformed and produced two reports.

The Majority Report, inspired by the Charity Organisation Society, condemned the work of Boards of Guardians and the indiscriminate and excessive use of outdoor relief. It recommended that Boards of Guardians should be replaced by district **public assistance committees** where individual casework would be encouraged as a key strategy in dealing with poverty with organised local charity aid available for the needy. Existing workhouses, which were 'often ill administered and normally demoralising',[2] should be replaced by new institutions each catering for the separate category of inmate. The alternative Minority Report, championed by Beatrice Webb and her husband Sydney, both members of the Fabian Society and one of the founding organisations of the Labour Party, advocated more radical change. It criticised the continuance of the workhouse, noting they were 'everywhere abhorred by the respectable poor' and that they had a 'positively injurious effect on the character of all classes of inmates, tending to unfit them for the life of respectable and independent citizenship'.[3] It emphasised the

Life in the Workhouse

We have ourselves witnessed terrible sights. We have seen feeble-minded boys growing up in the workhouse, year after year, untaught and untrained, alternatively neglected and tormented by other inmates . . . We have seen idiots who are physically offensive or mischievous, or so noisy as to create a disturbance by day and by night . . . living in ordinary wards, to the perpetual annoyance and disgust of the other inmates. We have seen imbeciles annoying the sane, and the sane tormenting the imbeciles. We have seen half-witted women nursing the sick, feeble-minded women in charge of babies, and imbecile old men put to look after boys out of school hours. We have seen expectant mothers, who have come in for their confinements working eating and sleeping in close companionship with idiots and imbeciles of revolting habits and hideous appearance.

(Beatrice Webb, member of the Royal Commission on the Poor Laws and the Relief of Distress, 1909)

economic causes of poverty and the need for the state to take action against unemployment. Arguing for the repeal of the Poor Laws, the Minority Report recommended that local committees should be set up to deal with specific types of poverty: issues of child poverty by an education committee; the sick by a health committee; and the elderly by one with a remit for pensions. It acknowledged that unemployment was a wider national issue and a government Ministry of Labour should be established with a network of labour exchanges to help the unemployed find work. But neither report was acted upon. The split decision within the Commission was an important reason why the government took no direct action. Nevertheless, their work ensured the issue of poverty remained at the forefront of public debate.

When the Reports were published in 1909 the political, ideological and social landscape was beginning to change. A new Liberal government, encouraged by a landslide victory in 1906, was pursuing its own programme of social-welfare reforms to combat poverty in childhood, or as a result of low pay, unemployment, ill health and old age. There was also a gradual move away from a laissez-faire approach by central government that they should not intervene in the lives of citizens or the workings of the market economy.

The ideological shift in political opinion was the result of a number of factors. In 1906 nearly four out of five males over the age of 21 were eligible to vote. The Reform Act had extended the franchise,

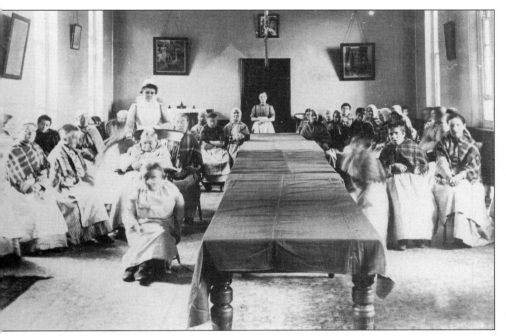

Gateshead Union Workhouse, 1906. Gateshead's first poorhouse was built in the grounds of St Mary's churchyard in the seventeenth century. When the Gateshead Poor Law union came into existence in 1836 a new workhouse was erected to house 276 inmates drawn from its 9 constituent townships. It soon became clear that this building was not adequate and after several extensions a new workhouse was proposed. After much debate a site was selected at High Teams Farm and opened in 1890. The workhouse, built to accommodate 900 residents and a school for 300 children, later became known as the 'High Teams Institution' and inmates are seen here. (Reproduced by permission of Gateshead Council, Libraries & Arts)

redistributed constituencies and, with secret ballots, made elections fair and transparent. Each of the major political parties adapted their policies to appeal to a larger, and working class, electorate. Disraeli's 'one-nation Toryism' envisaged the state taking a role in protecting workers from exploitation, while the Liberals were demanding an even greater role in employment and social issues. Moreover, trade unions and, by 1903, an organised and funded Labour Party had thrown down a challenge to the other parties to confront the problems of poverty.

Secondly, the work of social investigators, in particular Booth and

Rowntree and those who publicised the plight of the poor, had engendered a greater understanding of the problem. The laissez-faire view of poverty was that it was due to failings of the poor themselves. However, Booth in London and Rowntree in York had established that the extent and nature of poverty was not solely the consequence of individual weakness. They had both demonstrated by scientific method, independent of each other and at opposite ends of the country, that some 30 per cent of the population lived in poverty and through their analysis had showed the causes were low pay, ill heath, unemployment and old age, rather than idleness or fecklessness.

The third reason was due to concerns for national efficiency when Britain was challenged by its international rivals. Its greatest rival, Germany, already had a system of social insurance and pensions in place and, along with other countries, had established a network of labour exchanges for the unemployed. Even Britain's former colony New Zealand had introduced a pension scheme. Fourthly, the Boer War provided evidence of the consequences of poverty in Britain. Over 80 per cent of Army volunteers from the industrial towns and cities were victims of a poor diet and malnutrition and rejected as physically unfit for military service. Even politicians who had once paid little attention to poverty were now confronted with evidence that Britain had problems competing with other countries and retaining her dominant position in the world.

The Liberals did not come to power with a coherent programme of reform and were not working to any pre-determined plan. Although there was a general desire to reform the way government tackled poverty, Liberal welfare measures were introduced in a piecemeal fashion, as a result of political pressures, the work of individual members of parliament (not just of the Liberal Party) and even the skills of adroit civil servants.

The alarming fact that men at the start of the twentieth century were unfit for war service gave rise to the Government Inter-Departmental Committee on Physical Deterioration of 1904 which identified poverty in childhood as a source of unfitness in adults. This led to the introduction of the Education (Provision of Meals) Act in 1906 which allowed local authorities to provide schools meals for children in need. It was a Labour MP who proposed free school meals, but such was its popularity in the country that the Liberals adopted the measure. There was opposition to the scheme from those who believed it undermined parental responsibility. Amongst them was the COS who maintained it would have the effect of 'permanently demoralising large numbers of the population' and lead to the break up of families as parents lost the incentive to provide for their children.[4] Nevertheless, the Act set a precedent in allowing the state to make provision for something previously a family responsibility. It set another: by not disenfranchising the parents of the children concerned. One of the causes of the stigma felt by those claiming Poor Law relief had been the withdrawal of a claimant's right to vote. This was based on the notion that those who took from the state, and not contributed to it, did not earn full citizenship. With a wider acceptance of the causes of poverty the government now recognised the poor in need of state benefits were entitled to retain their full rights as citizens.

If the provision of free school meals arose from the concerns of a member of an emerging opposition party then the next measure, to address the effects of childhood poverty, came from within the government's own civil service. In the non-contentious, but detailed, Education (Administrative Provisions) Act of 1907, the Permanent Secretary at the Board of Education, Sir Robert Morant, who, according to one historian, 'was unimpressed by the radicalism of his political masters and decided that he would make things happen despite them', buried in the small print the recommendation for school medical inspections.[5] This was later followed by circulars from Morant to local education authorities, not only regulating the inspections but also authorising them to provide medical treatment.

Like school meals, the provision of medical inspections and treatment were at first permissive only. Neither were they something the Liberal government had planned for but, by 1914, over 14 million meals a year were being provided to 158,000 needy children and most local authorities had established clinics to cater for their medical needs.

The first intended reforms by the Liberal government were to curtail child neglect and introduce residential centres for juvenile criminals. The 1908 Children Act imposed penalties on parents who abused or neglected their children. Private children's homes were also registered and the Poor Law authorities made responsible for visiting and supervising the young victims of cruelty or neglect. The legal system was also reformed with the introduction of Juvenile Courts and children were separated from adult criminals with the decision to build residential Borstals for young offenders (see Chapter 8).

One of the major causes of poverty was an inadequate wage but this was not easily legislated against. In a free-market economy wage rates could only be set by the laws of supply and demand. Government intervention by setting minimum wage rates was seen as a step too far when it might endanger a firm's financial viability and cause unemployment in its workforce. In 1889, dockworkers went on strike for 6d an hour which ended in victory and added impetus to the trade-union movement. At the start of the twentieth century trade unions had become a powerful force for improvements in wages and working conditions. By 1903 there were 670 trade unions with fewer than 20,000 members apiece, but within 7 years their combined membership had grown to 3.1 million. The vicissitudes in the economic wealth of the nation, however, affected wage rates and put them beyond the sphere of influence of early trade-union negotiators. After 1900 national wage rates stopped growing and the cost of living increased. Retail prices rose by nearly a third in the first decade of the century, while the real value of wages fell by 13 per cent.

However, low wage rates endured by workers in non-unionised, so-called 'sweated' trades had been revealed as scandalous and could not be ignored. In 1908 a Select Committee Report on Home Work reported:

> if 'sweating' is understood to mean that work is paid for at a rate which, in the conditions under which many workers do it [then] the earnings of a large number of people – mainly women working in their homes – are so small as alone to be insufficient to sustain life in the most meagre manner, even when they toil hard for extremely long hours. The consequence is that, when these earnings are their sole source of income, the conditions under which they live are often not only crowded and unsanitary, but altogether pitiable and distressing.[6]

The most vigorous lobbying for a minimum wage came from a pressure group called the 'Anti-Sweating League'. This was formed in reaction to the Commission's Report and, at the instigation of the *Daily News*, a Sweated Industries Exhibition was staged at Queen's Hall, London. This dramatically demonstrated the hardships and distress of sweated labour. A spate of investigative reports on home work resulted from the publicity and accentuated pressure on the government for action.

The first Trades Board legislation was in direct response to the effects of the Anti-Sweating League campaign. Comprising employer representatives, workers, trade unions and government agencies, the

Boards set minimum wages and operated a social policy that assumed responsibility for the economic welfare of home workers. When the Act first took effect in January 1910 it established minimum wages for 200,000 workers, paid by the hour or according to output ('piece' rates) in the tailoring, paper-box-making and lace-making industries. In what was a significant shift from the lassez-faire attitude of the nineteenth century, the government also intervened to set minimum wage levels for miners in the 1912 Miners Act.

Despite trade-union interventions and the advent of Trade Boards, over a quarter of adult working males in 1906 received less than 20s a week in wages (worth about £57 today). For those who worked in agriculture, life was a particular struggle. There were more men than work available. The situation was reflected in the wage of farm workers. 'Wanted – Carter for farm work, wages £20 per year with board and lodgings. Apply Heath Farm, Great Rollright, Chipping Norton', ran an advertisement in the *Worcester Journal* at the start of the century.

Unemployment at the start of the twentieth century was a major cause of poverty and hardship. In 1908, 7 per cent of the workforce, or 800,000 people, were out of work. By then a more enlightened view of unemployment was gaining ground. The old belief that individuals were to blame for their failure to find work was being replaced by a new thinking that they needed help to identify what work was available and financial support while unemployed. To achieve the first of these aims the 1909 Labour Exchanges Act was introduced intended to promote the availability of work. By 1910 83 labour exchanges had been established and at the outbreak of the First World War nearly 2 million workers were registered at 430 exchanges. Although the war would later soak up increasing numbers of the unemployed who responded to Kitchener's call to arms, by 1914 over 3,000 jobs a day were being found within the national framework of labour exchanges.

The second plank in the Liberal's armoury in its fight against unemployment was a scheme to support and maintain those out of work. The Poor Law, with its system of workhouse-centred relief, was no longer seen as appropriate to deal with the issue of unemployment. Trade-union and friendly society insurance schemes were too selective in their membership criteria and for the lowest paid and unrepresented workers there was no help at all. The Liberal's solution was to establish an unemployment insurance scheme which, under the National Insurance Act of 1911, provided compulsory unemployment insurance cover for around 2.25 million workers in trades prone to seasonal or cyclical unemployment, such as construction, shipbuilding and engineering. This was funded by a tripartite arrangement where employees paid 2.5*d* a week into an insurance fund, the same sum was matched by employers while the state contributed 1.6*d*. Benefits of 7*s* a week were paid out to unemployed scheme members who were entitled to one week's benefit for every five contributions paid up to a maximum of fifteen weeks. Those who lost work through misconduct or left employment voluntarily forfeited their benefits.

The National Insurance Act also included provision for health insurance. In the early 1900s around 7 million people made their own arrangements, either through friendly societies or as members of a trade union, to cover medical costs. However, when met with rising food prices and increases in the cost of living generally not all were able to maintain payments and they let their policies lapse. Moreover, poor people, unable to pay the weekly subscription, were not insured at all and faced a grave crisis when illness debilitated a wage earner, for a lack of affordable medical care. Only applying to certain industries, for example, engineering and construction, the scheme was funded by national-insurance contributions and cost male workers 4*d* a week (females 3*d*), employers 3*d* and the state 2*d*. In return, benefits included free medical treatment, an entitlement to 10*s* a week sickness benefit (7*s* 6*d* for women) for the first twenty-six weeks of sickness, a disability payment and 30*s* maternity benefit. All workers aged between 16 and 70, earning less than £160 a year, were required to join the scheme with employers deducting contributions from pay.

Heath insurance was one of the most ambitious measures of Liberal social reform, but also the most contentious. Forcing employees to contribute led to resentment. Employers argued too against the time and cost of deducting contributions from pay. Doctors, under contractual arrangements with friendly societies, objected to becoming what they perceived as state employees. Friendly societies felt threatened by its existence, as did commercial insurance companies which feared a loss of profits in the face of state competition. Furthermore, when everyone paid the same level of contribution, regardless of income, the lowest paid lost the highest proportion of income. Despite opposition, by 1914 over 13 million workers were members of the scheme, and for those, to some extent, poverty caused by ill heath had been alleviated. Neither did it, as some feared, signal the end of private mutual-aid organisations. Their cumulative experience provided them with the central role as 'approved societies' to collect contributions and pay benefits on behalf of the government. This arrangement continued until 1948 when legislation combined the various state benefits into one unified system administered by central government.

The health-insurance scheme, like unemployment benefit, was a product of a Liberal reform programme. But the most enduring measure was pensions for the elderly. In the nineteenth century one of the most tragic images of poverty was that of the elderly living out their last years in the harsh confines of the workhouse. By 1900, however, the picture had begun to change. Many of the aged poor were receiving outdoor relief and for those with no home of their own, conditions in the workhouse were more relaxed. Nevertheless, this did not prevent campaigners seeking alternative, more appropriate methods of helping the aged poor. One of the first proposals for a non-contributory pension scheme was put forward by Charles Booth in the 1890s. But this was opposed on the grounds of cost. At an estimated £16 million it was more than the entire Poor Law expenditure and suggested at a time when the Boer War was already draining public finance.

By 1908 there was a broad consensus for some form of old-age pension. The newly formed Trade Union Congress, along with the Labour Party, supported the campaign. Even the COS – who once opposed its introduction believing that thrift and saving were the keys to financial security in old age – accepted the need for a pension scheme. The government had first considered a state pension in 1906, but upon the accession of the more radical Herbert Asquith as Prime Minister, and the similarly minded David Lloyd George as his Chancellor, they were also pushing for wider social reform.

The 1908 Old Age Pensions Act introduced a weekly non-contributory pension of 5s, payable to those over the age of 70. Initially, however, it had certain pre-conditions. It was only paid when income from other sources was less than 8s a week. Where income was greater than this it was reduced on a sliding scale and those on more than 12s got nothing. It was denied to anyone who had been imprisoned in the previous ten years, or had claimed poor-relief in the last two and to those who had habitually failed to seek work when they were under the receiving age.

Within 12 months of its introduction, 650,000 people were claiming a state pension and by 1915 the number had risen to 1 million. According to Lloyd George, 'it relieved a mass of poverty and destitution which is too proud to wear the badge of pauperism'.[7] There is little doubt pensions were popular. In her book, *Lark Rise to Candleford*, Flora Thompson recalls the reaction of her elderly neighbours:

> When the Old Age Pensions began, life was transformed for such aged cottagers. They were relieved of anxiety. They were suddenly rich. Independent for life! At first when they went to the Post Office to draw it, tears of gratitude would run down the cheeks of some, and they would say as they picked up their money, 'God bless Lord George (for they could not believe that one so powerful and munificent could be plain 'Mr') and God bless you, miss! And there would be flowers from the garden and apples from their trees for the girl who merely handed them the money.[8]

The amount of pension was by no means generous when it only matched what was a usual payment of outdoor poor-relief. The minimum age at which it was paid was harsh when many recipients were unfit for work in their sixties. Furthermore, by excluding ex-offenders it continued the increasingly outdated view that there were still classes of 'deserving' and 'undeserving' poor. It was, according to one historian, 'a pension for the very poor, the very respectable and the very old'.[9] Nevertheless, for those eligible it was a welfare benefit without the stigma associated with the Poor Laws. Moreover, the government's decision to fund a non-contributory pension scheme out of general taxation was seen as a novel means by which the state responded to poverty.

The social impact of the First World War only served to confirm a need for the state welfare-reform measures introduced in the pre-war period. In October 1914 the government began to pay family allowances to members of the armed forces. And a year later pension provision was extended to the widows and orphans of those killed in the war and, by 1916, unemployment insurance was available to most of the workforce. A Ministry of Labour (one of the recommendations of the Minority Report in 1909) was established in 1917, taking over the labour functions of the Board of Trade, and in 1917 a Ministry of Health was created to replace the Local Government Board.

During the war years the cost of living increased, as did wage levels, and the number of unemployed fell. This mini-boom, which extended into the immediate post-war years, encouraged the government to expand its pension scheme to men over 65 and women at 60. It also introduced the Unemployment Insurance Act of 1920 which gave protection to nearly all workers barring agricultural labourers and domestic servants. Theoretically, unemployment protection had been extended to 12 million workers. However, by the early 1920s the trend in economic growth was reversed. By disrupting the international economic order the war had hastened the rise of competition and adversely affected Britain's predominance of the world's financial and trading markets. These disturbances proved long lasting and the country's weaker international position was aggravated by stagnation in industries and regions where much of the nineteenth-century industrialisation was based. Together with fluctuations in the worldwide economy, it resulted in mass unemployment, prolonged periods of hardship and embittered social distress. Economic theory was turned upside down. Unemployment, it proved, was neither temporary nor self correcting. The problem was exacerbated in 1931 by an economic depression, augmented by the Wall Street Crash, which resulted in over 2.5 million being put out of work. Major industries that had been the main exporters in the nineteenth century struggled in the post-war years and throughout the 1920s and 1930s. The period is dominated by popular memories of unemployment, but it was regional in its nature. Nearly three-quarters of males were denied work in the coalfields of south Wales; in Glasgow four times as many were unemployed compared with the English Midlands; and in the shipbuilding centres of the north east 68 per cent were unemployed compared to 4 per cent in the London Home Counties.[10]

The scale of unemployment shook the local system of public assistance and transformed it. When local areas were unable to support the burden of local taxes the Poor Law broke down under the strain. It was also in disarray when sympathetic Boards of Guardians paid benefits more generous than the official entitlement, while others conformed to central government's continuing demand to minimise expenditure. In 1929 the government responded by introducing the Local Government Act which, in many respects, brought about the measures proposed by the Royal Commission's Minority Report in 1909. It abolished Boards of Guardians and disbanded Poor Law unions, replacing them with local **Public Assistance Committees** which became responsible for poor-relief; the workhouse test was ended and the former workhouses transferred to local authorities either as hospitals or as Public Assistance Institutions to accommodate the 'feeble-minded' unable to support themselves.

The burden of unemployment also undermined the existence of the national-insurance scheme. Successive governments in the 1920s introduced various measures in an effort to make and mend. Benefits were cut, contributions increased and a means test introduced in attempts to ensure the scheme remained viable. Despite these measures by 1931, when there were 2.6 million unemployed, the national insurance fund was £115 million in deficit. The system staggered on until 1934 when the Unemployment Act restored the benefits cut, but reduced the length of time over which they were paid. The Act also extended the scheme to include agricultural workers and replaced the Public Assistance Committees with an Unemployment Assistance Board, a central authority that finally removed local-authority responsibility for the unemployed and the able-bodied poor.

At the start of the twentieth century, when the Liberal Party was drafting its welfare reforms, Lloyd George jotted down a note: 'Insurance necessarily temporary expedient. At [a] not distant date [the] State will acknowledge full responsibility in the matter of making provision for sickness, breakdown and unemployment'.[11] It would be another forty years before that 'full responsibility' came to fruition.

Whatever the privations – from blackout to food control and censorship – there was full employment during the Second World War (never achieved in the 1920s and 1930s) and steadily rising wages ensured a relative improvement in the economic position of the lower wage-earning population. It bred a new optimism for the post-war years. 'The pre-war experience of a "bitter society"', one historian wrote, 'was turning people towards the vision of a better society'.[12] This vision of a new, revitalised, socially conscious Britain was encapsulated in a report published in 1942 entitled *Social Insurance and Allied Services*. Its author, a civil servant and later (briefly) MP, William (later Lord) Beveridge, attacked what he saw as the five giants of idleness, ignorance, disease, squalor and want; and put forward a programme for overcoming them not only with a comprehensive social-insurance system, but also economic policies designed to maintain full employment, a national health service and a 'new deal' in housing and education.

The report met with a cool response from Whitehall and from a government preoccupied with 'winning the war', but it proved overwhelmingly popular with the British public and more than 70,000 copies were sold in the space of a few days. The weight of public opinion was instrumental in creating the only major parliamentary revolt of the war years and forced the government to commit itself to the Beveridge proposals – with the result that they became the blueprint for the welfare-state legislation of the immediate post-war period.

In 1946 a newly elected Labour government introduced the National Insurance Act and two years later the National Heath Service Act. Far more comprehensive than its 1911 predecessor, the National Insurance Act, with its flat-rate contributions, covered, without exception, sickness, unemployment, industrial injury and old age: it provided 'a shield for every man, woman and child against the ravages of poverty and adversity'.[13] Its companion, the Health Act, although controversially and bitterly contested at the time, created a universally free at point of use health service. Meanwhile, a third piece of legislation, the National Assistance Act, was introduced to provide a safety net for the needy and began with the dramatic words 'the existing poor law shall cease to have effect'. Relief was now to be paid through a National Assistance Board and financed from direct taxation, rather than as a neighbourhood-rated scheme. This created a break not only with the 1834 Poor Law, but also the 'old' Poor Law of 1601. In 1948, as the Poor Law disappeared, replaced by a system of state benefits and a 'cradle to grave' health service, there was an optimistic belief that 'the poor would no longer be with us'.[14]

Chapter 8

DESTITUTE CHILDREN –
A CASE STUDY

'they were too ragged, wretched, filthy, and forlorn,
to enter any other place'
Charles Dickens, 1838

The wretched conditions that existed in the cities of industrial Britain were no more sharply defined than by the sight of thousands of homeless and destitute children, barefoot and ragged, haunting the alleyways and sleeping in doorways. There was no childhood for these street urchins. They relied on their wits, crime or prostitution for food and survival; those who lacked these abilities died. They were the product of parental bereavement and neglect, or employed as beggars and thieves by an indifferent – if not desperate – poverty stricken family. But it was not a problem unique to the age of industrial Britain.

As early as 1597 parish officers were required to arrange **pauper apprenticeships** for orphans and the children of paupers, since this relieved the parish of the cost of supporting them. Children were apprenticed from the age of 7 purportedly to masters, such as farmers or tradesmen, to learn a trade but were, in effect, seen as cheap labour. The 'mystery and art' of husbandry or housewifery were very commonly stated as the 'trade' to be taught. Many children were simply used as servants in the houses of labourers and smallholding farmers.

Apprenticeships were often organised by rotation and when a parish wanted to bind a child, the parishioner they had chosen as master had to take the boy or girl or pay a fine to be excused. In effect the apprentice became a member of the master's family. If a master owned or leased land in a parish and lived elsewhere the apprentice had to live there too; if the master moved from parish to parish the apprentice moved with him. If the master died, the apprentice could stay with his widow or be assigned to another master. Some landowners who were allocated apprentices assigned them to their tenants. Pauper apprentices had little protection from ill treatment or overwork in conditions that were often little better than slavery.

Such conditions became all too apparent by the eighteenth century when parish officials made agreements with industrialists to supply children in return for work and lodgings. At Styal in Cheshire, Samuel Greg, owner of the Quarry Bank Weaving Mill, took children from workhouses as far afield as London and East Anglia. Accommodation for 100 children was provided in an apprentice house where, although living conditions were harsh and the discipline strict, they were under the wing of one of the more enlightened employers. Here, children were cared for by Greg's own physician, fed from the cottage garden and offered opportunities to advance their status in the mill. George Courtauld opened a silk mill in Braintree Essex in 1809 and, when they were thought to be more obedient than boys, employed only girls between the ages of 10 and 13 years. Under an arrangement with parish workhouses he received £5 for each child, binding them to the mill until they were 21 years of age.

In the cotton industry alone, over a third of all workers were children, many of whom were pauper apprentices. Sarah Carpenter arrived at Cresbrook Mill in Derbyshire when she was aged 8. Like many other apprentices, she was treated appallingly by her employer:

> The master carder's name was Thomas Birks; but he never went by any other name than Tom the Devil. He was a very bad man – he was encouraged by the master in ill-treating all the hands, but particularly the children. Everybody was frightened of him. He would never let us speak. He once fell poorly, and very glad we were. We wished he might die. They was an overlooker called William Hughes, who was put in his place whilst he was ill. He came up to me and asked me what my drawing frame was. A little boy that was on the other side had stopped it, but he was too frightened to say it was him. Hughes started beating me with a stick, and when he was done I told him I would let my mother know. He then went out and fetched the master in to me. The master started beating me with a stick over the head till it was full of lumps and bled. My head was so bad that I could not sleep for a long time, and I have never been a sound sleeper since.[1]

In an attempt to stamp out the more inhumane practices, the Health and Morals of Apprentices Act of 1802 limited working hours for pauper children to 12 hours a day, required a minimum standard of accommodation and the provision of an elementary education. The enforcement of the Act, however, was in the hands of local magistrates who, either factory owners themselves or under pressure from influential friends, failed to ensure compliance and the Act was largely ineffectual.

In 1848 it was estimated in London alone that 30,000 shelterless children were running wild. In the same year, when prisons were still tenanted by the very young, 15,000 juvenile law-breakers and vagrants shared filthy, unsanitary cells with hardened criminals where the strongest ruled and the predatory rounded on the weak. The sheer numbers of a young, unruly criminal element was the cause of concern. The social commentator Matthew Arnold refers to 'this vast residuum . . . marching where it likes, bawling what it likes, breaking what it likes'.[2] Child poverty and its link with crime was a challenge to those who strove to provide these waifs and strays with an education in the hope it would enable them to lead honest and virtuous lives.

Education facilities were strongly defined by class. Grammar schools, originally intended for the children of the poor, were taken by the wealthy and the privileged. Governesses were employed by those able to do so, or mothers taught their children to read and write, but for the working classes there were few schools. Those that did exist were run by charities, religious organisations – notably the Quakers – or by single women at home, usually at a weekly charge, known as dames' schools. Few were prepared to accept the 'ragged' child whose dress, attitude and demeanour were the result of grinding poverty and destitution. As Charles Dickens was to note, 'they were too ragged, wretched, filthy, and forlorn, to enter any other place'. His exposure in *Oliver Twist* of the reality behind the Poor Laws and the London that lay beyond the knowledge of society did much to encourage the growth of schools for the poor.[3]

There is debate about who started free education for destitute children. History is littered with individuals who selflessly gave time to teach 'ragged' children. Robert Raikes, appalled at children's behaviour on the Sabbath, is credited with starting the Sunday school movement in 1780. And sixteen years earlier the Revd Theophilious Lindsay had opened a school in Catterick, Yorkshire, and, inspired by Lindsay, a Mrs Cappe opened a Sunday school at Bedale in 1765.

Undoubtedly, a number of other well-meaning individuals, independent and perhaps in ignorance of each other, had also started to teach. The term 'ragged school' was not applied until 1843 when *The Times* newspaper described the Field Lane School in Holborn, London, in this way. The actions that led to the growth of **ragged schools** can be attributed to the work of three particular people – John Pound, a Portsmouth cobbler, the Revd Thomas Guthrie in Scotland and the 7th Earl of Shaftesbury, Anthony Ashley Cooper.

John Pound, unable to pursue his trade as shipwright when an accident rendered him disabled, began teaching young waifs and strays in Portsmouth the three 'R's (reading, 'riting and 'rithmetic) and gave lessons in carpentry, nature study and shoe-making. His reputation as a teacher grew and he continued to teach destitute children until his death in 1839, but it was a Free Church of Scotland minister who championed the cause and publicised Pound's work.

Thomas Guthrie was born in Brechin in 1803 and was ordained in the ministry of Arbirlot, Forfarshire, in May 1830. After his appointment as Moderator of the Free Church General Assembly he turned his attention to the plight of Edinburgh's homeless destitute children. According to C J Montague, Guthrie became interested in ragged schools after seeing a picture of Pound in his cobbler's shop: 'he was there himself, spectacles on nose, an old shoe between his knees, that massive forehead and firm mouth indicating great determination of character, and from between his bushy eyebrows benevolence gleamed out on a group of children . . . all busy at their lessons around him'.[4] In 1847, acknowledging Pound's work, Guthrie wrote the pamphlet 'Plea for Ragged Schools' and opened three schools that catered for 265 children. Although one of the most well-known moderators of the Free Church of Scotland, he would – according to his son and biographer Charles – have simply been content to be remembered as the apostle of ragged schools. While Guthrie became a protagonist in Scotland, 400 miles away in London one of the leading evangelical philanthropists of the nineteenth century was to also hear of ragged schools.

Elected Member of Parliament for Dorchester in 1830, Lord Ashley, later the 7th Earl of Shaftesbury, led a successful campaign for factory reform and a shorter working week. In a speech at Sturminister Newton in 1843, he criticised many of his landowning constituents for their ill treatment of labourers and tenants. His sympathies for the oppressed led to him resigning his seat in opposition to his party's position on the Corn Laws. This gave him the opportunity to become involved in a number of philanthropic activities, including his endeavour to pursue, for moral and spiritual reasons, an improvement in the education of children.

By 1844 nineteen ragged schools had opened in London, and a meeting held at St Giles's School in Bloomsbury resulted in the Ragged School Union being formed. William Locke, its first secretary, gave evidence to the Standing Committee on Criminal and Destitute Juveniles in 1852 and explained the reasons for the Union:

> we were very anxious indeed to have another class of schools in London at that time, and we thought it an excellent plan to have a Union so that we might arrange plans, and assist each other in carrying out so desirable an object as to that of gathering in the outcast and destitute who were idling or doing mischief in the streets.[5]

When Locke gave evidence there were 195 day schools, 209 evening schools and 272 Sunday schools affiliated to the Ragged School Union.[6]

Maybole Ragged School, Ayrshire, Scotland

Maybole Ragged School in Ayrshire was founded by a group of benefactors with subscriptions from the town's inhabitants. It was run by a committee that aimed to remove as many waifs and strays from the streets of the town as finances would allow, and to educate them in the four 'R's (reading, 'riting, 'rithmetic and religion). In the mid-nineteenth century, the local Church of Scotland minister, and also a committee member, compiled a register of the children, and recorded the meetings.

Entries from the register

William Martin Coburn
Aged 13 years whose father is dead was in the habit of begging both in town and country could read none was bought to school upon the 12th of Feb 1849. At which time he had nowhere to lay his head his mother at that time being confined in the county prison for theft. William at the beginning appeared to be a stupid dull boy and to have a very narrow ignorant mind but as he increased in learning the mist of ignorance soon disappeared. He was also a very quite boy and appeared to be very happy at school for the space of four months. His mother at this time being liberated from prison thought it more profitable to have him at the begging. Accordingly upon the 14th of July she took him from school notwithstanding his unwillingness to

go he travelled the country with her for the space of three weeks he then left her and came back to school at which he remained to the 15th of Feb 1850. He then caught fever and lingered a few weeks and departed this life. Previous to his death he was a good reader in the bible and he appeared to understand what he did read.

Samuel Thomson
14 years of age was bought to school upon the 16th of July 1849 this boy was well known to be a notorious thief and a public beggar, and his father being dead his mother had no control over him; therefore he went on from one evil to another. When he came to school he was ignorant as a heathen. Neither knowing a letter nor a God I used all the means in my power to tame this savage but all was in vain. I think he deserted school 18 times; the last time he deserted school was upon the 4th of June 1851; and upon the day following he was taken before the magistrates of Maybole for some act of theft; the sentence was passed on Samuel for this crime was one night in prison and banishment out of Maybole. When Samuel left school he was a good reader.

The minutes

Convened the following members of the Acting Committee on the 6th of Feb 1850
Reverend Mr Dodds
Mr M Brown
Mr R McMillan
Mr Murdoch
Mr Hannay
The teacher reported that the case of Helen McCafferty was bought before the Parochial Board when it was arranged that she is to continue in the ragged school and be maintained for one year at the rate of one shilling and six pence per week for food and education.
The Meeting then took into consideration other claims lodged for admission to the School on behalf of children since last meeting when it severally considered. The Meeting refused the claim for admission of Mary Fisher's son (14 years of age and can read a little). They admit Agnes Heggart's child on condition of paying 2d per week, not charging the first week and paying it each a Monday. They admit Hugh child of Helen Fisher for one month and on condition that he ceases to beg and if found begging to be dismissed. They admit Mrs Henderson's child on condition of paying 4d per week. Messrs Murdoch and Hannay reported that they had visited their District for subscriptions and had obtained in whole £6-10s.

(Reproduced by permission of Maybole Community Council)

Locke's submission to the committee provides the best understanding of what life was like in the East End of London in the nineteenth century and a clear appreciation of the need for ragged schools:

> When they are first taken into the schools, most of them are ignorant, destitute, neglected condition, many are quite homeless; many neglected by their parents; many are orphans, outcasts, street beggars, crossing sweepers and little hawkers of things about the streets. We have children of convicts who have been transported, children of thieves in custody, children of worthless drunken parents, a large class, children of parents, though honest, are too poor to pay even one penny a week for a school, and who cannot clothe their children so as to obtain admission to better schools; children who have lost their parents, or deserted by them, or have run away from home and live by begging and stealing, children who are at work during the day and who therefore cannot attend day school, even if free admission be offered . . .[7]

Although not all schools were affiliated to the Union, its establishment provided much-needed publicity, helping provide financial support and offers of assistance. It also acted as an advisory body, able to give practical help and grants to those wishing to start a school. Shaftesbury requested a meeting 'so that I may discover for myself the scope of the work and how it may be extended'.[8] Those attending included George Holland from the George Yard Ragged School Mission in Whitechapel and the Salvationist Catherine Booth. The meeting led to the Ragged School Union gaining Shaftesbury as their chairman; a position he held for thirty-nine years until his death in 1885. Under Shaftsbury the number of schools affiliated to the Ragged School Union grew and by 1869 there were 195 day schools, 209 evening schools and 272 Sunday schools, with an average attendance of 26,000 pupils. There was one other member present at the meeting whose name was to become became synonymous with the plight of destitute children.

Irish-born Thomas Barnardo moved to London to study medicine at the London Hospital with the intention of becoming a missionary for the China Inland Mission. But, disillusioned with his medical studies, he turned his attention instead to the plight of homeless 'Street Arabs'. With the discovery of young Jim Jarvis (who died for want of shelter) was the realisation of the scale of the problem. Barnardo was often

Off Street Ragged School, London, 1865

Quintin Hogg (1845–1903), a successful merchant and philanthropist, started Off Street (later York Place) Ragged School, Charing Cross in 1864. The following extract is taken from *Quintin Hogg a Biography*, written by his youngest daughter Ethel and published in 1904 by Archibald Constable & Co.

> The boys used to come into the house in an indescribable condition, so that it was absolutely necessary to shave their heads and literally scrub them from head to foot before they were fit to associate with any human being; all of which unpleasant operations Mr Hogg used to perform with his own hands. The class prospered amazingly; our little room, which was only 30ft long by 12ft wide, got so crammed that I used to divide the school into two sections of sixty each, the first lot coming from 7 to 8.30, and the second lot from 8.30 to 10. There I used to sit between two classes, perched on the back of a form, dining on my 'pint of thick and two doorsteps' as the boys used to call coffee and bread and treacle, taking one class in reading and the other at writing or arithmetic. Each section closed with ten minutes' service and prayer.

quoted as saying that his first few months in London did more to open his eyes to the miseries of the poor than at any other time.

The hopelessness of destitute children encouraged Barnardo to give a speech at a missionary conference where he gained the support of a number of benefactors. As a result, he was able to open his East End Juvenile Mission in 1868. Barnardo's unambiguous approach to fundraising – unheard of in the nineteenth century – included taking a photograph of every child he had rescued and again a few months later, and he then sold the 'before' and 'after' cards in packs of twenty for 5s. His later policy of never closing the door to destitute and orphaned children led to an ever-increasing demand for beds. By 1878, over fifty orphanages had been built, including a village of seventy cottages for girls, complete with church and school, at Barkingside in Ilford, Essex.

Ragged school teachers, mostly working voluntarily, came from various backgrounds and often undertook the rescue and recruitment of children off the streets by following Shaftsbury's advice to 'stick to the gutter' in finding the poorest first. The school day comprised lessons in the three 'R's, and for some children, an opportunity to wash, receive food, boots and clothing. To remove any temptation of parents to sell or pawn any item, clothing would be stamped with the name of the school. For many the daily routine included Bible lessons, and for some schools donated Bibles were the only means of teaching reading and writing. Industrial classes were often included; the girls learning domestic skills, the boys, carpentry, brush-making and shoe-making. In Liverpool clogs were made, and a printing press available to print bills for tradesmen and bags for grocers. In some cases it was food not education that was the first requirement when the simple but wholesome food would often consist of soup, occasional meat, bread and milk, coffee and cheese. Readers of the church magazine *Home Words* were encouraged to make donations towards an annual Christmas dinner for ragged school children; an event so successful that by 1896, upwards of half a million destitute children had been fed. Mothers' clubs were created enabling mothers to go out to work, and the School Dinners Association formed – a forerunner of school meals. Day trips to the country and the seaside were arranged. The 'Fresh Air Fund' was set up by the editor of *Pearson's Weekly*, inviting his readers to pay for a day's holiday in the country for those attending ragged schools.

The gradual decline of ragged schools began in 1870. An Education Act of that year required that all children attend school from the age of 5 and local school boards were established to train teachers and set educational standards. Regulations were introduced for buildings and ragged schools, with a lack of funding, were unable to meet these and as a consequence they began to close. Many of the poorest children, unable to afford school fees, went without an education until fees were abolished in 1891. In 1910, sixty-six years after the Ragged School Union was founded, the last school closed.

Ragged schools were not without their critics. One dissenting voice was that of Henry Mayhew, an investigative journalist who wrote regularly for the *Morning Chronicle* about how the poor of London lived and worked. He argued 'since crime was not caused by illiteracy, it could not be cured by education . . . the only certain effects being the emergence of a more skilful and sophisticated race of criminals'.[9] Another was Mary Carpenter, the daughter of a Unitarian minister, who in 1846 opened a school in Bristol for homeless children 'on the borders of a criminal or vagrant life'.[10] Appalled by the behaviour of the more 'difficult' child, she published the pamphlet 'Reformatory Schools for the Children of the Perishing and Dangerous Classes and for Juvenile Offenders'. In it she argued that children should be removed from the environment that encouraged criminal behaviour and their potential reformed by training 'in the habits of industry'. Quite possibly unknown to Carpenter, her views were shared by a Chairman of Prisons Board 540 miles away in Aberdeen.

Alexander Thomson was a keen supporter of Aberdeen's Industrial Feeding School, which had opened in 1846. On its first day of operation the police were said to have rounded up seventy-five children who were found begging and in some cases literally carried off to the school. The children were forcibly washed and then given three substantial meals a day. The school was supported by voluntary contributions and employed paid staff. The idea was to get children into the school at an early age before they had the opportunity to form bad habits. Most were taken under 11. The routine at the school was a mixture of lessons, industrial training and feeding. By 1851, when the number of schools had grown to four, Thomson was claiming that their advantage over English ragged schools was in the employment of full-time staff which allowed the children to be supervised all day, seven days a week.

The Ragged School Union opened its first 'Juvenile Refuge and Home of Industry' for homeless children in 1847, before adding a further fifteen by 1856. By then **industrial schools**, intended to help children who were destitute but had not committed any serious crime, had opened throughout England, Wales and Scotland. These, like the ragged schools, were run on voluntary lines until the introduction of the Industrial School Act in 1857. This provided magistrates with the authority to commit vagrant children, between the ages of 7 and 14, to a school, usually some distance from an area that was known to them. Extending these provisions in a further Act in 1861, children found begging, receiving money or food given as charity to the poor, in the company of thieves, consorting with prostitutes or 'whose parents declare him [or her] to be beyond their control' were also committed to an industrial school. The Act also stated the child had to be 'apparently' under the age of 14. This was because children often lied about their age if it was advantageous to do so and some genuinely did not know how old they were. It was not until 1855 that it became compulsory in Scotland to register births.

Although an alternative to prison, life in an industrial school was a harsh and a sometimes cruel existence. The daily timetable was strict. Children rose at 6.00 am and went to bed at 7.00 pm. Between these times there were set periods for schooling, learning trades, housework and religion in the form of family worship. The boys learned trades such as gardening, tailoring and shoe-making; the girls, knitting, sewing, housework and washing. There was also a strict punishment regime for any misdemeanour when children forfeited privileges, were deprived of a meal, kept in solitary confinement or for more serious of offences, six strokes of the birch.

Not all schools maintained such a harsh regime. The Exeter Girl's Industrial School and Servants Home was established in 1861 to train girls as domestic servants. Managed by a committee of six ladies, the home accepted neglected and destitute children and taught them the rudiments of housework as well as 'habits of order and obedience'. Young girls who 'had lost their situation through incompetence' were amongst those accepted in the school.[11] The age of admission was between 13 and 16, although girls of a younger age were admitted if paid for at a rate of £10 a year and if they had their clothes supplied. An individual, who believed children should be saved from a life of destitution, established an industrial school that seemed to have a happier, more contented prospect. Wealthy William Gillum, after a distinguished Army career, bought a farmhouse in the Middlesex town of Barnet and started a school that was home to a hundred boys. Under Gillum's tutorage the boys kept chickens, sheep and cows and delivered milk and fire wood to nearby homes. In addition to a basic education lessons included chess, singing and playing the piano. When they left at 16, boys with no local family connection either emigrated to Canada and Australia or others, not surprisingly, joined the Army.

The most infamous of all industrial schools were the Magdalene Laundries, operated in Ireland by the Sisters of the Magdalene Order and brought to prominence in 2002 by the film *The Magdalene Sisters*. Orphaned destitute girls, 'guilty of illegitimacy', pregnant or simply too pretty – and therefore in 'moral danger' – were put to work in convent laundries without pay to 'wash away their sins'. Stripped of their identities, the girls were given numbers instead of names. They were forbidden to speak, except in prayer, and beaten severely if they tried to escape or broke any rule. The last laundry did not close until 1996 and it has been estimated that during a period of 150 years over 30,000 women where subjected to this brutal regime.

When poverty was inextricably linked with crime, it was the government's Youthful Offenders Act of 1854 that recognised law-breakers under 16 as a separate group. This gave magistrates the authority to send youngsters to a reformatory school. The first reformatory in Britain was established in 1836 on the site of the present-day prison at Parkhurst on the Isle of Wight and intended to train boys who were under sentence of transportation for two or three years before their removal from this country. In 1852 a parliamentary committee was established to 'inquire into the condition of criminal and destitute juveniles in the country, and what changes are desirable in their present treatment in order to supply industrial training, and to combine reformation with the due correction of juvenile crime'.[12] Thomas Guthrie was summoned from Scotland to give evidence and in one of his answers laid the basis for reformatory schools. 'What I contemplate is first a ragged school for the purpose of catching children before they reach prison; and then a reformatory school for the purpose of telling upon children who have already become criminals'.[13] The result was Lord Palmerston's Act of 1854 which accredited **reformatories** and importantly funded then out of public assets. They grew rapidly; by 1859 when the 'Reformatories and Refuge Union' had been formed there were over ninety in existence in England and Wales and fourteen in Scotland.

In the nineteenth century Britain's heavy reliance on its naval fleet for trade and defence saw destitute, orphaned and delinquent boys as willing, or unwilling, candidates for a life at sea. In response to a shortage of volunteers, the Marine Society was born and during the French Seven Year Wars provided over 10,000 boys for naval service. Having met the demands for war service, the Society commissioned a small merchant ship, the *Beatty*, and moored her at Deptford, as the world's first pre-sea teaching ship, and started to train boys for the Royal Navy and the merchant services. In 1862 it obtained the loan of a larger vessel from the Admiralty to accommodate 200 boys; renamed *Warspite*, this, and a succession of vessels traditionally carrying the same name, trained and equipped more than 70,000 boys before the last ship was decommissioned in 1940.

The *Beatty* was one of the first of a number of ships to provide accommodation and training at various locations around the British Isles. The Malone Reformatory, established in 1860, had at its disposal the Admiralty vessel *Gibraltar*, moored off Carrickfergus in Northern Ireland, for use as an industrial school between 1872 and 1899. In Scotland, on the River Clyde, two **training ships**, first the *Cumberland* and then the *Empress*, became a familiar sight for generations of Glaswegians. Ships moored on the River Mersey included two reformatory ships, the *Akbar* for Protestant boys and the *Clarence* for

'A Walk Round the Ragged School'

There is upwards of 20 ragged schools distributed throughout the poorer districts of the town [of Liverpool] in which almost 3,000 children of the most destitute classes are receiving gratuitous instruction. By far the most interesting is the Industrial Ragged School in Soho St. The conditions which children are rejected in other schools render them eligible for this, bad character, filthiness, ignorance and crime; these are the best possible passports for admission.

The number of pupils are 96, with an average attendance of 85, the school opened in March last year and is aided by donations from the Ragged School Union, its maintenance £500 a year. At the moment only boys are admitted, but money is being raised to open a like accommodation for girls. Since the opening, on the first anniversary two months ago, 228 children have passed through. Of these, 108 were born in Liverpool, 79 in Ireland, 41 other places. 54 were orphans, 73 had only mothers, 15 had been deserted, 112 beggars and 4 known thieves.

With the exception of two schools in Toxteth Park, supplied by a benevolent Lady [a resident of the Dingle] of food twice a week, the Soho St School is the only establishment providing food and education. The pupils are provided with three meals a day, at a cost of a half-penny a meal or 1s-1d a week per head.

Breakfast – oatmeal porridge and treacle.

Dinner – three days, pea soup, three days rice (which, we are told, the boys find insipid)

Supper – a slice of dry bread sprinkled with salt (to give it relish)

New scholars unaccustomed to regular meals cannot eat all the food at first, but their appetite gradually grows.

This is the only school where industrial operations are carried out. The boys are not taught trades, 'we studiously avoid that,' said the Superintendent cordially – we could only stare at his comment in disbelief. All that is desired is to impress them with the value and importance of labour, and impart the habits of industry.

The mornings are devoted to study, the afternoons to recreation and work. The chief industrial occupations are, tailoring, clogging, knitting and netting, there is also considerable manufacture of paper bags.

A Tailor on a moderate salary is employed, under his tuition the boys have mastered the mysteries of lapboard and scissors, and they are able to repair their own garments with neatness and skill. Then under the instructions of a competent craftsman, the scholars repair old shoes into decent looking clogs, and every pupil is furnished with a pair. They were busy on our visit with 100 pairs, ordered by an anonymous benevolent, intended as a gift to other schools.

An old lady who fills the office as cook, and has scholars as assistants, volunteered to teach the younger boys knitting. A good many nets were made first and boar bristles are sorted by the younger boys into black and white.

There is a printing press lent by Mr MC CORINDALE, the persons ordering the paper bags can have their names printed on them if they wish.

There is a spacious playground attached to the premises and owing to the enforced cleanliness and recreation permitted, the children are kept in excellent health. Although they sleep at home, such 'homes' as they may have are situated of necessity in the worst districts of the town, the institution has not lost any inmates to the Cholera, and since opening only one death has occurred of measles.

Lavation is not neglected; 15 lbs of soap are consumed weekly. There are baths to which newcomers on admission are immediately introduced. Their linen is duly washed, for very few of the poor wretches can boast of a change of clothing, the most destitute are provided with clothing in a very coarse fabric.

Those who attend school on Sundays, (two thirds do) are rewarded by being allowed to don a sort of blue smock like frock. The walls of the store room are adorned with smart articles of clothing from benevolent donations.

The school was once made an instrument of swindling, a Lady appeared showing a warm interest in the institution and her sympathy took a practical shape, she took it on herself to call at the houses of the Gentry, pleading for donations of all kinds to benefit the school, she was very successful, and sent some of the gifts, the committee were overjoyed. It at length transpired that the Lady had embezzled and appropriated to her own use, all the donations of great value, Mr RUSHTON, intervened and terminated the fraud.

A dozen of the boys besides being boarded and educated are also lodged at the house provided for the Industrial Master in the neighbourhood of St Michaels Church.

The little fellows were found a night at the Night Asylum by two benevolent gentlemen connected to the institution. Dreading the influences of the hard felon, recounting his feats of imposture and fraud, they resolved that whatever the cost, to snatch the poor homeless children from the possibility of vagrancy and crime.

The boys are apt scholars and the most grateful and orderly boys. The education at the school consists of the usual plain elements. There is a library, formed exclusively of some 50 volumes of religious tracts.

Among the pupils we found entered in the books, we found a, James HUGHES, aged 14, a native of Manchester, for some time he has resided at Crosbie St in this town. A short time prior to our visit he was bound apprentice, and had gone to sea. He was one of the first pupils in the school and had displayed great skill in manufacture. He was a great favourite with the boys, and when he left the parting was romantically affecting. One scholar gave him a souvenir in the shape of a button and another, a rusty knife.

The establishment is under the superintendence of Mr J. B. ORRISS, eminently qualified for the delicate and arduous task, the boys treat him with readiness and respect.

Every department of the school is governed by love and the happy results are everywhere visible.

(Quoted from the *Liverpool Journal*, 1 June 1850; reproduced by permission of the administrator of the *Old Mersey Times* website)

Catholic boys. There was also the *Indefatigable* used by the Liverpool Sea Training Board after John Clint, a Liverpool ship owner, founded a charitable institution to train orphaned and destitute boys to become merchant seamen. In 1945, the *Indefatigable* merged with the Lancashire and National Sea Training Homes, which had, since established in 1896, provided an orphanage for 'British boys of good character, health and physique, regardless of religion or poverty'.

Thomas Barnardo, using his considerable influence, established a shore-based ship where his orphaned boys could receive nautical training. With the help of wealthy ship owner, Edmond Watts, he was able to purchase the former Norfolk County School near Fakenham in Suffolk and with conversion complete, the 54-acre Watts Naval Training School was almost self-contained with its own gym, laundry, chapel, games room, playing fields, sanatorium, staff accommodation and even a cemetery.[14] The pupils for this land-based sea-training school were specially selected from homes managed by Barnardo, and would arrive by train, disembarking at the school's own railway station. The school provided many sailors for service with the Royal Navy, and continued to provide naval training until 1949, when the facilities were transferred to Parkstone Nautical Training School in Dorset, although the buildings continued as a **Barnardo home** until 1953.

In 1910 voluntary bodies undertook the main provision for the 30,000 children in all 37 reformatories and 90 of the 112 industrial schools with the Home Office retaining powers of inspection and certification. The legislation introduced in the mid-nineteenth century for destitute and delinquent children remained in force until the Children Act in 1908. During the First World War, many institutions were taken over for military use as hospitals and sold at the end of hostilities. Reformatory and industrial schools survived until 1933 when they combined to form a single category of 'approved' schools, but by then those detained had fallen to 6,000. With education being provided by the state, the treatment of young offenders necessitated change. The next and final stage in the development of reform schools centres on a village, the name of which has become synonymous with youth offending.

The Kentish village of Borstal, 1½ miles south-west of Rochester, was the site of the first school – and henceforth carried its name – that offered a programme not only of education and regular work, but also a strict regime of character-building activities. Opened in 1902, Borstal was one of a number of detention centres that continued to operate until the introduction of the Criminal Justice Act in 1982, when they became Young Offenders Institutions.

In 1884 Parliament enacted the Poor Law Adoption Act that allowed Boards of Guardians to send destitute children to the colonies. Although the first-known, organised **child migration** occurred in 1618, when a group of 200 boys left Britain for America to work on the tobacco plantations of Virginia, it was not until the second half of the nineteenth century that the majority of migration schemes were put in place.

Over the next one-hundred years, until the final group embarked for Australia in 1967, an estimated 150,000 children had been transported to Canada, Australia, South Africa and other parts of the Empire. Whatever the later doubts, during the nineteenth century the work of individuals, charities and Poor Law authorities in arranging migration for these 'street urchins' was applauded. It was seen as a way of rescuing children and at the same time solving the social, economic and moral problem of child destitution.

One of the first migration schemes was that of retired naval captain Edward Brenton, who founded the Society for the Suppression of Juvenile Vagrancy in 1830. He opened two schools, the Brenton Juvenile Asylum in Hackney Wick and the Royal Victoria Asylum (for girls) in Chiswick. In 1832 he sent the first party of children to the Cape of Good Hope and the Swan River Colony in Australia. Renamed the Children's Friend Society, it was later to send 230 children to Ontario and New Brunswick. In those early days long-distance sea voyages were perilous affairs with high mortality rates, and it was the relatively short distance to Canada that attracted others to emulate his work.

Canada, with its vast expanse of sparsely populated areas, had an urgent need for agricultural labourers. With the support of the British government, the Home Children Movement officially started in 1869 when the Canadian government offered £2 for each child exported from Britain. One of two people to start emigration on a substantial scale was Maria Rye, described as a 'formidable woman who at times seemed hostile to the children in her care', who had taken an active role in promoting employment opportunities for women.[15] Persuaded to transfer her energies to the emigration of 'gutter children', the first party of seventy-five girls, aged between 4 and 12 at Kirklade Industrial School, embarked from Liverpool for Canada on 28 October 1869. With the financial support of the Poor Law authorities and grants from the Canadian government, Rye established a children's home in Peckham, London, and a receiving home in Canada. Despite disturbing reports regarding the lack of aftercare that her children received in Canada, and accusations of profiting personally, she continued her work until retiring in 1895. Rye's more-compassionate contemporary, Annie Macpherson, had by 1868 established, with Church support, her 'home of industry' in Spitalfields after being appalled by the conditions in which local homeless children made matchboxes. The home provided the children with food, shelter and an education, before they embarked, under her care, to a new life in Nova Scotia. Between them, these two women, of differing temperaments and backgrounds, had by the turn of the century arranged the emigration and adoption in Canadian homes of nearly 12,000 children.

Others too played a part in the emigration of children. The Children's Society (formally the Waifs and Strays Society), with initial support from Poor Law relief, was actively involved from 1883 to 1955 in arranging migration of children to Canada, Australia and Southern Rhodesia. In 1871, William Quarrier started an orphanage and farm school in Scotland, from where children went to Canada under the supervision and care of Macpherson. Kingsley Fairbridge, living in Rhodesia, followed his dream by establishing farm schools: 'Train the children to be farmers, he exhorted, not in England, teach them their farming in the land where they will farm . . . shift the orphanages of Britain to where farmers and farmers' wives are wanted'.[16] It was, however, Thomas Barnardo who, influenced by the work of Annie Macpherson, took a major role in child migration.

In the 1880s, Barnardo enthusiastically supported sending orphaned children to start a new life in Canada. He recorded in his journals: 'We in England, with our 470 inhabitants to the square mile, were choking, elbowing, starving each other in a struggle for existence; the British colonies overseas were crying out for men to till their lands, with few ties to bind them to the mother country, and at an age when they were easily adaptable to almost any climatic extremes'.[17] In 1882 the first party of Barnardo boys, supplied with a 'Canadian outfit' – comprising a Bible, *Sankey Hymn Book* and suitable clothing – left Liverpool for Canada. His emigration programme gained momentum and each year thousands of destitute children collected together at 'the great export emporium' in Stepney before embarkation. Answering the call for domestic helpers, the first of many groups of Barnardo girls set sail from Liverpool in 1883. Construction of the railways opened up new areas of previously uninhabitable land for farming settlements, and with it an insatiable need for cheap labour. Barnardo established a number of homes in Canada and employed a retinue of staff to receive, process and dispatch children to various farm settlements, largely in the isolated Dominions. The arrival of a ship, transporting upwards of 400 children, 4 times a year, would be met by press announcements inviting Canadians to secure the services of a Barnardo boy or girl. In exchange for bed and board, children were apprenticed for seven years and worked as farm labourers or domestic servants, and on reaching the age of 14 years, were expected to negotiate a monthly wage. In a new venture, Barnardo bought several acres of land in Manitoba and on it built an industrial farm where older boys were taught farming skills. After eight months training, boys left to start their own homesteads.

Despite the understanding that food was plentiful, work abundant and schooling freely available to all, it was a harsh and sometimes brutal experience for these young settlers. Concerns of ill treatment were often considered unfounded, after all, it was argued, life could be no worse than anything they had previously experienced. After a life in Britain, however short and desperate, many found living on an isolated Canadian farm a challenge, with houses miles apart, the weather, the people and the environment, all foreign to their urban upbringing. With the best intentions of Barnardo and his staff monitoring placements, reports surfaced of maltreatment and punishment beatings. For some Canadians, like their English cousins, who believed that poverty was the product of the person rather than

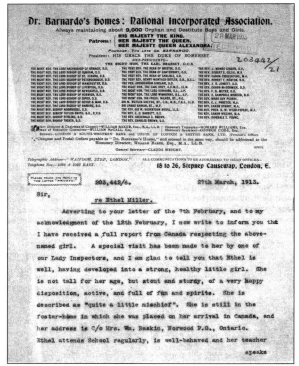

A letter written to an unknown recipient regarding the welfare of one Ethel Miller, who, at the start of the twentieth century, was under the care of Dr Barnardo.
(Reproduced by permission of The National Archives (Ref: HO144/1118/203442))

circumstance, 'home children' were treated as hired hands, not to be trusted or considered equal. According to one of Barnardo's employees, 'some were prejudiced enough to imagine that by taking one of these [children] into their households they are incurring the risk of having their throats cut in the night or waking to find their barns in flame'.[18] In these difficult conditions there were young suicides and absconders, but many more survived to become farmers in their own right, or to succeed in professions far removed from that which brought them to Canada. It is estimated today that 'home children' and their descendants represent 11 per cent of Canada's population. Child migration continued until the outbreak of the Second World War, when it was estimated a total of 90,000 children had been sent to Canada. It was then that migration societies turned their attention once again to Australia.

Australia had been a destination for child migrants since the eighteenth century and, like Canada, the Australian government was keen to populate the country with 'good, white British stock'. The original aims were encapsulated by the Fairbridge Society, which established a farm in Western Australia in 1912 to provide training in agriculture for boys and domestic service for girls. With financial assistance from the Overseas Settlement Board, Fairbridge bought a farm near Perth and started to receive groups of children, but it was not until after his death in 1924 at the early age of 39 that the farms expanded. This was a model later followed by the Catholic Church, Barnardo's and the Salvation Army during the inter war years. In post-war Britain, the need for child emigration changed, the welfare state had begun to care more for the destitute and the Children's Act of 1948 placed a greater emphasis on keeping children within a family setting. Those children who did migrate to Australia were those offered for adoption and placed in orphanages and institutions.

The Catholic Church became involved in child migration in 1926, when it established an Order of Christian Brothers orphanage for boys in Western Australia. This was followed by a second at Bindoon, a sprawling 17,000-acre industrial farm near Perth. The treatment meted out to the boys was harsh and cruel, with sexual abuse and starvation commonplace. The boys received a scant education, but instead were put to work constructing many of the buildings themselves. The isolation of these farms, in the remote outback, ensured the harsh conditions remained unknown for much of their lifetime. It was to have a lasting effect on many. One ex-Christian Brother, who saved a number of boys from drowning, was later to admit 'it might have been better if the creek had claimed them, in view of the terrible life many ultimately led'.[19] The Salvation Army, which in the nineteenth century had assisted children to migrate to Canada, had by 1920 established a training camp near Brisbane to house orphaned children, many of whom were bought to Australia on vessels chartered by the Army.

In September 1939, the British government established the Children's Overseas Reception Board, enabling a number of children to emigrate to Canada and the United States for the duration of the Second World War. Many of the 15,000 children selected were housed in the industrial farms and orphanages of the Fairbridge Society and Dr Barnardo's. The scheme came to a tragic end in October 1940 when the *City of Benares*, carrying ninety children to Canada, was torpedoed and sunk crossing the Atlantic, claiming the lives of all but seven on board.

In 1946, the Fairbridge Society, by then based in London, established the Fairbridge Memorial College in Bulawayo, Southern Rhodesia. But this was to be different from the industrial farms of Canada or Australia – the Rhodesian government encouraged child immigration, but with the aim of achieving white supremacy. The College provided children with career opportunities in industry and public service. The selection of pupils matched these expectations with intelligence and social standing viewed as important attributes. When children left at 16, they were found work and issued with no more than a train ticket

Dr Barnardo and the Custody of Children

JUDGEMENT AT THE HOUSE OF LORDS

The House of Lords this morning gave judgement in the appeal case of DR BARNARDO-V-FORD.

This was an appeal from an order of the Court of Appeal of the 27th January 1890, affirming an order of the Court of Queen's Bench of the 30th November 1889, making absolute a rule nisi for a writ of habeas corpus, commanding Dr BARNARDO to bring up the body of Harry GOSSAGE, a boy of 12 years of age.

The boy was the son of Mary FORD, having been found in a homeless and destitute condition by a Police Constable at Folkestone and was received into Dr BARNARDO'S Home through the interposition of the Rev Edward HUSBAND a clergyman at Folkestone, on the 25th September 1888

It was alleged on the part of Dr BARNARDO that the father who died some time previously was a Wesleyan Methodist, and his mother was a woman of drunken habits, who constantly neglected him.

In November 1888, Dr BARNARDO transferred the care of the lad to Mr William NORTON, to be taken to Canada. About the same time an application was made to Dr BARNARDO on the behalf of Mary FORD for the production of the boy in order he may be placed in a Catholic Home in Harrow Rd.

The lad was then in the care of Mr NORTON and had been taken to Canada.

Legal proceedings were taken which resulted in the orders referred to above, against which Dr BARNARDO appealed.

Their Lordships dismissed the appeal with costs.

Mr RIGBY. Q.C, made an application for an extension of time to return to the writ. Their Lordships, after consideration, fixed the return at three months from the present date.

July 1st 1892

(Quoted from the *Liverpool Echo*, 25 July 1892; reproduced by permission of the administrator of the *Old Mersey Times* website)

and voucher to exchange for clothing. For many, in a foreign country and without family or friends outside the isolated confines of the school, it was a daunting experience. Some have since returned to Britain, but others remained in what is now Zimbabwe. The College received 300 children from Britain before it closed in 1955.

Those engaged in child migration believed that removing children from orphanages or the destitute from the streets to rural surroundings in a new country would improve their life and prospects. Many survived the transition, but no account was taken of the effect on the child, or the manner in which they were selected. As one Barnardo boy would later recall: 'Kids in those days were regarded as a little less than human. They were sent to countries for economic reasons. It couldn't have been for the children's sake. Not if they had any sensitivity at all'.[20]

After the Second World War, and in a more enlightened society, children arrived in Australia with the knowledge and support of at least one living parent remaining in Britain. With a post-war increase in marriage breakdowns and illegitimacy, unwanted children were placed in homes for adoption, with parents supporting their child's migration. After 1947, natural parents had enrolled more than half of the children arriving in Australia under the auspices of the Fairbridge Society, which, until closing its homes in 1955, sought wherever possible to send siblings together and encourage children to retain contact with family relatives.

SEARCHING FOR POOR
AND PAUPER ANCESTORS

Appendix 1

GETTING STARTED

First steps

Researching your family history isn't always easy. You'll be looking for clues, asking questions, finding blind alleys, and yes, there will be a lot of dead bodies along the way. But with a bit of luck and a lot of patience you will run your man to ground. This is no truer than when searching for a poorer ancestor. Such was the stigma attached to poverty – when the widely held belief was that it was the result of an individual's own idleness or unreliability – that families were not readily able to accept or discuss a relative's reliance on poor-relief, their removal to the workhouse or as a recipient of charity aid. The poor too felt shamed. In Chapter 5 we read of young Charles Shaw's experience of entering the workhouse when he wrote of the family, 'we went by the field road to Chell, so as to escape as much observation as possible'.[1]

You may well of course not know at the outset that you have a poor or pauper ancestor when they only come to light as you work your way back through the centuries. As with family history research generally, start with what you know and write it down and then see what your relatives have to contribute. Family anecdotes, recollections and reminiscences may provide clues to an ancestor's position and wealth in society. Talking to the oldest of your closest relatives should be a task that is never delayed. It is my lasting regret that I was unable to discuss a branch of the family's history with my maternal grandmother when as a child I heard her – all too often it seemed then – recall without hesitation a seemingly intricate web of past family relationships. You will find that once people start to think over events of the past, memories often come flooding back about things that had long been forgotten. It is a sad truth that some of the older generation are ashamed of their origins, particularly if they came from a poor background and you may find that they are reluctant to divulge too much about their parents or grandparents. Even in the recent past attitudes towards divorce and illegitimacy were very different from those of today.

What you are told by an elderly relative may not always turn out to be the truth. Many a family has a romantic tale that hides a reality. 'Of course, you know that Uncle Mac, your great great grandfather's brother, ran away to join the circus', I was once told, which may be a tale born more out of fiction than fact. Whether or not he was a rich man, poor man, beggerman or thief the story may well have been an invention that, quite innocently, has been passed down the generations to hide some dark secret. Perhaps he was a villain of sorts and transported to the colonies, or removed in disgrace by the overseer to another parish, or entered a workhouse, or did indeed join the circus when smitten by the charms of some lion tamer's daughter! But then again, a favourite way for a young man to avoid paying the parish for the upkeep of his bastard child was to run away to join the Army or the Navy.

The Internet

The Internet had revolutionised family history research. It is now easier than ever to find information or share an interest with others. Most family history societies have their own website and there are an estimated 20,000 mailing groups devoted to genealogy. National, metropolitan and local record offices, together with local study centres, also have online facilities. These are posting transcriptions of primary records, or at least indexes of them, on the Internet seemingly by the minute. Poor Law records are particularity well served in this way. The Access 2 Archives (A2A) search engine (www.nationalarchives. gov.uk/a2a/) provides a link to provincial and national searchable databases that will enable you to identify ancestors who were, for example, served with removal notices, settlement certificates or bastardy bonds. Individual parish accounts can also be identified and located alongside details of the thousands of charities and philanthropic organisations that provided (or still provide) succour to the poor.

Such has been the growth of online genealogical material that information on sources is in danger of rapidly becoming out of date. The same can be said of website addresses. Those mentioned in the book were accurate at the time of going to press, but web pages come and go and if you find any that fail then the answer can often be found when using a search engine such as Google (www.google.co.uk). Alternatively, a particularly helpful book that lists useful websites is Peter Christian's frequently revised *The Genealogist's Internet*, published by The National Archives (see Appendix 3). One of the best places for family historians to start searching the World Wide Web is by using 'gateway' sites such as GENUKI (www.genuki.org.uk), which hosts a comprehensive collection of website links, not only to pages devoted to individual topics, but also to county record offices, national archives and local family history societies. If your genealogical interests extend beyond the British Isles then the equivalent website is Cyndi's list at www.cyndislist.com. You will not, however, find a great deal of information online about individual ancestors who were born in the twentieth century. It is only when you go back 100 years, and outside the scope of current privacy restrictions, that source material becomes available on the Internet.

I have assumed readers will have Internet access at home, but if you do not then many municipal libraries and local study centres have installed computers linked to the World Wide Web. Local education authorities also regularly provide computer (and family history) courses as part of their range of daytime or evening classes in 'leisure' and activity pursuits. That said, it is of course still perfectly possible to undertake family history without the use of a computer. But the principal advantage of the Internet, alongside its pages of help, advice and information, is that it offers the ability to check electronically on the holdings of record offices and libraries so that any visit can be better prepared and more productive. Family historians who live some distance from their ancestor's home parish, and therefore often the geographical location of any records, will particularly benefit when copies of documents can, for a modest fee, be ordered by post or email; the Internet, to quote from one website, provides 'a happy and fulfilling marriage between the virtual and the solid'.[2]

Where the records are

The convenience of the Internet does not replace the thrill of seeing and holding original records that mention, or were generated by, an ancestor. Moreover, the Internet can only be a guide to the availability of source documents, particularly so when many of the online transcripts and indexes are prepared by clerical staff without specialist training in palaeography. A general introductory guide to the terms and usage of English found in the early documents illustrated in the book can be found in, for example, Joy Bristow's *The Local Historian's Glossary of Words and Terms*. (See Appendix 3.)

Most of the surviving records of the poor are held in national, metropolitan and local record offices. The National Archives (TNA) at Kew provides a useful research guide to its records (Domestic Record Information Sheet 71) at: www.nationalarchives.gov.uk/. Similar help is available from TNA of Scotland at: www.nas.gov.uk/, and for Ireland on the website of TNA of Ireland at: www.nationalarchives.ie/.

Poor Law records

Parish officials were often very meticulous in their paperwork and as a result a great amount of information about the poor who received forms of 'outdoor' relief can be obtained from Poor Law documents. The most important of these are probably the accounts produced from the start of the seventeenth century by overseers of the poor, and later Boards of Guardians, for each parish in mainland Britain and Ireland. These were originally retained in the parish chest and contained a careful note of all money received and disbursed for poor-relief. Magistrates also took diligent care in recording evidence when punishing vagrants, adjudicating on poor-relief appeals, deciding on a pauper's right of settlement, issuing absconding fathers with bastardy bonds or drawing up pauper apprenticeship indentures. It should be noted, however, that the survival rate of records differs enormously between parishes – in some cases, very little remains. A directory of other archives holding Poor Law records in the United Kingdom and Ireland can be found at: www.workhouses.org.uk.

Charity records

It is a similar case with the private sector. Tens of thousands of national and local charities, together with mutual-aid organisations such as friendly societies, have existed – and some still exist – to provide succour to the poor and financial assurance for the lower paid. But until the early nineteenth century – when registers of charities were first maintained and private charitable endeavours better controlled – records were routinely destroyed when a charity went out of existence.

Records of charities that have survived can be found in parochial or subscription charity records deposited in national, county and metropolitan archives. For the period prior to 1841, you should also consult the reports of the *Commissioners for Inquiring concerning Charities* (published by HMSO in thirty-two volumes, between 1819 and 1840). This was an attempt to compile a comprehensive, geographically indexed description of all charities in England and Wales that were known of at the time. Copies of these reports are held in (or obtainable through) national, metropolitan and county record offices.

Newspapers

Newspapers are also an important – and often under-used – resource in any study of Poor Laws. It is unlikely that individual paupers will be mentioned, but appointments and resignations of officials often were. In local newspapers you are likely to find verbatim accounts of meetings of Boards of Guardians and accounts of visits made by local reporters to a local workhouse. National newspapers also took a keen interest in the Poor Laws, when, for example, *The Times* was at the forefront of exposing the Andover workhouse scandal. (See Chapter 5.)

Local record offices and local study libraries often have a collection of newspapers for their area. The largest collection of newspapers, however, is held by the British Library Newspaper Library (telephone: +44 (0)870 444 1500; website: www.bl.uk/. *The Times* Digital Archive is also available to view online at many municipal libraries.

Parliamentary papers, reports of Royal Commissions and other inquiries

Parliamentary papers are also a useful source in tracing pauper ancestors. The Parliamentary Archives at the House of Lords (telephone: +44 (0)207 219 3074; website: www.parliament.uk/publications/archives.cfm) has a complete set. Many university libraries also have copies that are obtainable through the inter-library lending service. A catalogue of British Parliamentary Papers is available at: www.britishparliamentarypapers.com/index.html.

Included in the series are the results of the Royal Commissions that were established to report into charities and the conditions of the poor. The most important of these were the two Commissions on the Poor

Laws, commencing in 1832 and 1905 respectively. The former Poor Law Commission's Report entitled *Copy of the Report Made in 1834 by the Commissioners for Inquiring into the Administration and Practical Operation of the Poor Laws* can be read in full online at: www.econlib.org/library/YPDBooks/Reports/rptPLC.html.

* * *

For a general introduction to the subject of family history readers should seek out a guide such as *Easy Family History* by David Annal, or the more in-depth *Ancestral Trails* by Mark Heber. (See Appendix 3.) There are also a number of family history magazines on the market such as *Ancestors*, *Family Tree Magazine* or *Practical Family History*, which regularly include articles devoted to various aspects of research or on topics of social and historic interest.

Appendix 2

THE RECORDS

Almshouses

Documentary sources for almshouses including minutes and admission registers etc. are mainly deposited in national, county or metropolitan record offices, although it may be worth contacting the charities that run almshouses first. You may also find descriptions of holdings on the A2A website at: www.nationalarchives.gov.uk/a2a/. Rossbret's website at: www.institutions.org.uk/almshouses/ may also provide historical data on a particular almshouse, together with its census reference number which will help trace residents. Details of those still in existence can be found at: www.charitiesdirect.com. Information and contact details of almshouses registered with the Charity Commission for England and Wales can be viewed at: www.charity-commission.gov.uk, or in Scotland at the Office of the Scottish Regulator at: www.oscr.org.uk/. The Victoria History of the Counties of England is yet another good source of information on almshouses and available online at: www.british-history.ac.uk. A complete set of volumes is held at TNA library and many local reference libraries also have sets. Not every county, however, is covered. Many almshouse charities have published their own histories, including information on current services and accommodation. The Durham Aged Mineworkers' Association, for example, on its website at: www.durhamhomes.org.uk/ includes a downloadable version of its history in north-east England. The Almshouse Association, which represents the interests of its member organisations, can be contacted at: www.almshouses.org/; telephone: +44 (0)134 445 2922.

Barnardo homes (see also Child migration)

Although Barnardo's no longer runs orphanages, its commitment to its founder's vision lives on. This includes its 'Making Connections' facility which is a national and international service providing access to Barnardo's personal and care records.

Making Connections also provides support, advice and intermediary services to adopted adults and former care adults. It also offers independent counselling and support to birth parents and relatives on behalf of several local authorities. In addition it can provide information and help with:

• Access to post-adoption services for adopted adults, birth parents and relatives;
• Accessing records for former care adults in Britain, Australia and Canada;
• Tracing family members;
• Intermediary services following successful tracing;
• Genealogy services for descendants of former Barnardo children in Britain, Australia and Canada.

Contact details: Making Connections, Barnardo's, Cottage 4, Tanners Lane, Barkingside, Essex, IG6 1QG 9; telephone: +44 (0)208 498 7536; email: makingconnection@barnardos.org.uk; website: www.barnardos .org.uk.

Bastardy

The circumstances surrounding an illegitimate birth generated a large amount of paperwork beginning with a bastardy examination of the mother-to-be. Every attempt was made to obtain the name of the father so he could be issued with a bastardy bond, or a warrant if he had absconded, ordering him to pay for the birth and the maintenance of the child. Bastardy bonds and maintenance orders may lead to the name of the father, when this is not mentioned on a parish or civil registration certificate, but also will state the amount of money the father was to contribute, together with the sex, date of birth of the child and where it was born.

Bastardy bonds, providing evidence as to the parentage of the child, survive in local county or metropolitan record offices. In the Shropshire archives, for example, there is a bond issued on 14 November 1778 recording that Mary Hyde, late daughter of John Hyde, gave birth to a daughter where William Palmer, a buckle-maker of Hockley Heath in Birmingham, is named as the father. The term 'illegitimate' was not used in parish registers until the eighteenth century, although the Latin *illegitima* is sometimes found. A natural and lawful son also may appear in Latin as *filus naturalis legitimus*. Many other terms were used for illegitimacy: bantling, base, base-born, bastardus, begotten in adultery, begotten in fornication, born extra, by-blow, by-chip, by-scrape, by-slip, chance begot, child of shame, love begot, lovechild, merrybegot, misbegotten, scape-begotten, spurious and whoreson.

Burial clubs

A search for records of burial clubs and societies can be made on the A2A website at: www.nationalarchives.gov.uk/a2a/. For example, at the Oldham Local Studies Centre in Lancashire (telephone: +44 (0)161 770 4654; website: www.oldham.gov.uk/community/local_studies .htm) there exists records of 'The Crown and Cushion Children's Burial Club' in Failsworth, which appears to have been formed in the 1870s at the Crown and Cushion public house to provide assistance for families towards the cost of burials of children.

Charity Commission (see also Trust deeds)

Enrolments of land given for charitable purposes are held at TNA at Kew in Richmond, Surrey. Enrolments made at the Court of Chancery and the Supreme Court of Judicature (from 1736 to 1925) as part of the Law of Mortmain are also held at TNA under class reference C54 and J18. Other historic and archival material relating to charities that has been selected for preservation is normally transferred to TNA no later than thirty years from the creation of the records. Amongst those already held (under TNA series CHAR2 and CHAR8) are near comprehensive surveys of charities that date between 1817 and about 1940. These contain a wealth of information on the activities and history of those organisations and, having the advantage of being indexed geographically, mention many private individuals. The Charity Commission has produced a paper 'Access to Charity Commission Records' which can be downloaded at: www.charity-commission.gov.uk/tcc/ccrecords.asp.

Further information on individual charities for the period prior to 1841 can be found in the thirty-two-volume reports of the *Commissioners for Inquiring Concerning Charities*, which is a comprehensive, geographically indexed description of all charities in England and Wales that were known of at the time. The entries are arranged by county and although they do not record who received benefits from a charity, do include details of the benefactor, the appointed trustees and a summary of the financial accounts. Copies of the reports are held in (or obtainable through) county and metropolitan record offices.

Charity Organisation Society (COS)

The records of the COS and its successor organisation, the Family Welfare Association (FWA), including the minute books of former district committees, are usually held in county record offices and, in the capital, at the London Metropolitan Archives. Investigation into individual cases was carried out by district offices and their records do include casepapers. These were normally destroyed after a case had been closed for twenty years, although it was not uncommon for a case to be open for thirty years. Examples of typical cases, omitting names, were published in the annual reports of the district committees which are also usually held in local county or metropolitan offices. All records of the FWA less than sixty years old, with the exception of annual reports and other publications, are closed to public consultation unless written permission for access is obtained from the Family Welfare Association (contact: telephone:+44 (0)207 254 6251; website: www.fwa.org.uk/).

Child migration

United Kingdom links

Barnardo's Aftercare Services holds a child-migrant index of over 30,000 children who migrated to Canada, plus the records of Macpherson Homes between 1882 and 1939. Access to the index and Barnardo's records generally is limited to proven descendants only (for contact details see Barnardo Homes above).

The Department of Health has produced a factsheet, 'Former British Child Migrants', which also provides contact details of all the various organisations involved in the migration of children (contact: DH Publications, PO Box 777, London SE1 6XH; telephone: +44 (0)300 123 1002; website: www.doh.gov.uk).

The National Archives at Kew has produced a research guide 'Emigrants – Domestic Records Information', which can be downloaded from their website at: www.nationalarchives.gov.uk.

Records of some organisations that sent children overseas are held by the University of Liverpool Special Collections and Library, Sydney Jones Library, University of Liverpool, PO Box 123, Liverpool L69 3DA (telephone: +44 (0)151 794 2696; website: sca.lib.liv.ac.uk/collections/).

The transcript of the (UK) Parliamentary Select Committee for Health into the Welfare of Former Child Migrants can be accessed at: www.parliament.the-stationery-office.co.uk/pa/cm199798/cmselect/cmhealth/755/75504.htm.

Canadian links

The Toronto Emigration Office holds registers of Barnardo children, information on known relatives and their settlement in Canada. The website, part of the Archives of Ontario, is at: www.archives.gov.on.ca/english/interloan/hawkes.htm.

The (Canadian) British Home Children website at: http://freepages.genealogy.rootsweb.ancestry.com/~britishhomechildren/ contains a database of over 50,000 child migrants and includes, for example, ages, country of birth and year of arrival in Canada.

Australian links

The National Archives of Australia has produced a factsheet on child migration, which can be downloaded at: www.naa.gov.au/about-us/publications/fact-sheets/fs124.aspx.

The Christian Brothers Ex-Residents and Student Services (CBERSS) website at: www.cberss.org/phind.html includes a personal-history index of former child migrants to Catholic homes in Australia between 1938 and 1965.

The Australian government's report on child migration and a Senate Inquiry can be downloaded from: www.aph.gov.au/library/intguide/sp/childmigrantuk.htm.

Co-operative movement

For many families, membership in the co-operative society was an integral part of daily life. Many will remember their parents', or grandparents', 'divi' number, or being sent to the 'co-op' for groceries. At the turn of the twentieth there were approximately 1,500 separate co-operative societies. Over the years these have merged together to form the forty consumer co-operative societies that operate today.

Located in Manchester, the National Co-operative Archives is home to a wide range of records relating to the history of the co-operative movement. The collections include rare books, periodicals, photographs and oral histories which provide researchers with a resource to trace the development of the co-operative movement from its inception in the eighteenth century to the present day.

Records of particular interest to the family historian include local society records, national publications (such as the *Co-operative News* and the *Scottish Co-operator*) and over 2,000 local society histories, published to celebrate jubilees and other anniversaries. These help illustrate how the organisations played an important role in the lives of ancestors and about the business and recreational activities that were open to them. There may be information here on individuals that were members of a co-operative committee or were officials in a local society. In most cases, however, the records do not extend to include an individual's membership or employment details. For further information, contact: National Co-operative Archives, Co-operative College, Holyoake House, Hanover Street, Manchester M60 0AS (telephone: +44 (0)161 246 2925; website: archive@co-op.ac.uk).

Emigration

The Poor Law (Amendment) Act of 1834 permitted Poor Law unions to supply money, clothing or goods to poor families for their passage to the colonies. This assistance continued until 1890, and it is estimated that, between 1836 and 1846 alone, Boards of Guardians assisted 14,000 English and Welsh families to migrate, especially to Canada. Records of the administration of the scheme, including correspondence and lists of pauper emigrants (arranged by county and Poor Law union), are at TNA, which has also produced a research guide, 'Emigrants to North America after 1776', which can be downloaded from their website.

Family Welfare Association (see Charity Organisation Society)

Friendly societies

It is estimated that at the start of the twentieth century one in two adult working males belonged to a friendly society. Fortunately, for the present-day genealogist almost all societies were required to submit rulebooks, sickness and mortality tables and accounts to the Registrar of Friendly Societies. These, which form the great mass of friendly society records, have been deposited at TNA, in series FS and cover the period 1785 to 1966. In addition, the Registrar's five-yearly reports from 1852, summarising much of the data provided by friendly societies, are available in the series of British Parliamentary Papers available at university libraries or through local municipal libraries.

Perhaps the most valuable for family historians are the minute books and membership lists kept by friendly societies. Sadly, some have been lost or destroyed when early societies were dissolved. However, many do remain, either in the archives of existing societies or deposited with local county or metropolitan record offices.

Searching the A2A website by place name and county will identify the county record office holding records of an individual friendly society, including in some instances a list of members. Similar results can be obtained by searching by the name of the society (for example, 'Independent Order of Rechabites').

A list of present-day friendly societies and their contact details can be obtained at: www.friendlysocieties.co.uk, which also includes a short history. The Association of Friendly Societies at: www.afs.org.uk also provides a list of its members and the financial products and services on offer.

The Annual Directories of the Independent Order of Oddfellows for the period 1845 to 1935, together with the *Oddfellows Magazine* from 1828 to 1935, have been microfilmed. These include biographical information on members, ceremonies and details of lodge activities, and are available for inspection either through county record offices or libraries.

The Ancient Order of Foresters has recently established The Foresters Heritage Trust and opened up access to the Order's archives of historic documents, regalia and artefacts. See their website at: www.aoforestersheritage.com/Index.html.

The Friendly Societies Research Group promotes research into the history of friendly societies at: www.open.ac.uk/socialsciences/friendly-societies-research-group/current-societies.php.

Industrial schools

In the absence of other information, census returns often hold the key to an ancestor's location at ten-yearly intervals from 1841 to 1901. This is also the case for those residents at an industrial school or detained in a reform school. Census enumerators delivered a return for completion to each superintendent responsible for a school. Pupils at reformatories are usually described as 'inmates under detention' and in industrial schools simply as 'pupils'. Magistrates, believing children needed to be removed from their home environment, frequently committed them to industrial or reform schools some distance from home. Under the Reformatory Schools Act 1854 and the Industrial Schools Act 1857, boards of governors were required to keep an extensive record of inmates and pupils. This task usually fell to the superintendent, who was also expected to complete a journal 'of all that passes in the school' and this would record admissions, where convicted or sentenced, licences (for day release), discharges and offences and punishment. These records are usually held in local county or metropolitan record offices. In the Devon Record Office, for example, there is an extensive collection of casebooks and registers from 1850 to 1960 (subject to a 100-year closure period). These contain the pupil's or inmate's name, age, where convicted, length of sentence, committal orders, medical certificates and dates of discharge. The Devon Family History Society (contact at: www.devonfhs.org.uk) has compiled an index of residents of the Devon and Exeter Boy's Industrial School for the period 1873 to 1888.

Information on all certified reformatories and industrial schools in England and Wales and much more (including in some instances a brief history and transcripts of census returns) can be found on Mary Wall's well-informed missing ancestors website at: www.missing-ancestors.com.

Training ships were used extensively not only as floating reform and industrial schools, but also by charity schools. Bernard de Neumann's website at: www.trainingships.royalnavy.co.uk/names.htm contains detailed notes of each vessel used.

Information about reformatories and industrial school by county, together with staff records, can be found on Rossbret's website at: www.institutions.org.uk/reformatories.

For a detailed analysis and complete list of Borstals, including detainees' own stories, visit the website at:www.borstal.skinheads .co.uk.

Ireland

There was hardly a facet of Irish life at local level upon which the Poor Law did not impinge and the records are one of the most important primary sources on life in Ireland from the early nineteenth to the early twentieth centuries. Irish Poor law records are held either at the Public Record Office of Northern Ireland, 66 Balmoral Avenue Belfast, BT9 6NY, Northern Ireland (telephone: (+44) (0)289 025 5905) or at The National Archives of Ireland, Bishop Street, Dublin 8, Ireland (telephone: (+ 353) 01 407 2300). Records are also held at local level. In the Clare County Library, for example, are the minute books of the Board of Guardians for the Ennistymon Union covering the period 1839 to 1850; contact: County Library Headquarters, Mill Road, Ennis, County Clare, Ireland (telephone: (+335) 065 684 6350).

The Northern Ireland Record Office has produced a series of information leaflets for the family historian, including 'Poor Law Records' available to download at: www.proni.gov.uk/index/research _and_records_held/catalogues_guides_indexes_and_leaflets/informa tion_leaflets.htm.

The National Archives in Dublin hold several very complete collections of workhouse records relating to the North Dublin Union, South Dublin Union and Rathdown Union (part of County Dublin and County Wicklow). As well as minute books, these collections include indoor registers which give the names and personal details of those entering the workhouse, as well as a wide variety of other records.

Ireland's National Archives also hold smaller collections relating to Balrothery Union (part of County Dublin), Bawnboy Union (part of County Cavan), Dromore West Union (part of County Sligo) and Lismore Union (part of County Waterford). The National Archives contain orders made by Poor Law Commissioners and Local Government Board, 1839–1921, and files of the Dail Eireann Department of Local Government, 1919–1923. A fuller description of records held at The National Archives of Ireland can be downloaded at: www.nationalarchives.ie/research/poorlaw.html.

Kirk sessions (Scotland)

The English and Welsh Poor Laws and acts of settlement did not apply to Scotland. Scottish paupers could apply for relief from charities from their parish (only if they were old, infirm, orphaned or destitute under the age of 14 years). Poor funds were raised by assessment on heritors (the principal landowners). poor-relief disbursed and monies received may be recorded in Kirk minutes. The National Archives of Scotland (contact: H M General Register House, 2 Princes Street, Edinburgh,

EH1 3YY (telephone: +44 (0)131 535 1314)) hold the records of Kirk sessions, which consist of accounts listing payments to the poor and appeals from parishioners from the refusal to grant relief. Full details of records held by The National Archives of Scotland can be downloaded at: www.nas.gov.uk/guides/poor.asp.

The Scottish Archive Network is a project aimed at revolutionising access to Scotland's archives by providing a single, electronic catalogue to the holdings of more than fifty Scottish archives. Included on its website at: www.scan.org.uk/familyhistory/myancestor/pauper.htm is a page devoted to Scotland's poor-relief records with a link to the SCAN Knowledge Base.

Parochial boards (Scotland)

In 1845, the Poor Law (Scotland) Act established parochial boards to administer poor-relief in each parish. Records of the parochial boards are held at the National Archives of Scotland or regional record offices and many include information on those who received poor-relief. Sheriff-court records will also include applications by officials for orders that fathers should support their illegitimate children or wives whom they have deserted.

Confirmation that Robert Muir was admitted to Stranraer Poorhouse on 18 May 1895. (Reproduced by permission of the National Archives for Scotland (Ref: CO4/33/6))

Parochial charities

Until the late nineteenth century most charities were of a local nature and limited to the parish or town where a benefactor lived or was born, and usually administered by parish officials. Records of these parochial charities can be found by searching the A2A website at: www.nationalarchives.gov.uk/a2a/. Here, for example, we learn that the Wiltshire and Swindon History Centre in Trowbridge (contact: telephone +44 (0)122 571 3000; website: www.wiltshire.gov.uk/leisure-and-culture/heritage/history-centre-project.htm) is the depository of charities in the Wiltshire town of Wootton Bassett, including 'Mrs Merryman's Coal Trust (Poor) 1856–1907' and 'The Rev John Wickes Charity (Poor) 1907–1931', both of which contain details of recipients who received charity relief.

Pauper apprenticeships

Apprenticeship indentures gave the name of the apprentice, his master and the parish to which the boy or girl belonged. Other information may include the name of the apprentice's parents, his or her age, the occupation of the master and the trade to be learned. Some of the early indentures list the things an apprentice must not do, including playing cards or dice or marrying without the master's consent. In return the master agreed to feed and clothe the child and teach him or her a trade, usually in return for a small sum of money. Most apprenticeships were for a term of seven years, but usually continued until the child was 21.

Two indentures were drawn up on one piece of paper, one above the other, and signed by the overseer (s), the master and two magistrates. The paper was then cut in half; one copy kept in the parish chest and other retained by the master, who presented it to the apprentice at the end of his or her term of service. Indentures could only be cancelled by the mutual consent of the three parties involved. However, in practice many apprentices did not stay with their masters. They were often badly treated and cases of abuse can sometimes be found in Quarter Session records. Others absconded and masters put advertisements about runaway apprentices in newspapers. Some parents refused to allow their children to be bound as apprentices and records of these disputes can survive in overseers' records. Although compulsory apprenticeship was abolished by the Poor Law Amendment Act of 1834, the system of parish apprenticeship did not finally end until the early twentieth century. Surviving indentures for pauper apprentices can be found in county and metropolitan record offices.

Poorhouse (Scotland)

Poorhouses or almshouses have existed in Scotland since medieval times, principally in burghs. Between 1845 and 1930 over seventy poorhouses were constructed in Scotland, many serving a number of parishes (called 'Poor Law unions' or 'combinations'). In 1845 the Board of Supervision issued detailed regulations for the records to be kept by poorhouse governors. They included a register of inmates with details, including the religious persuasion of each, a journal, which was an official log book or office diary, and a report book of offences against the rules of the poorhouse and punishments imposed. For many poorhouses all that survive are minute books of the managing committee or board, and these are usually found amongst county council or civil parish records held in local-authority archives. Substantial records survive for a few poorhouses; most notably those for Kyle Union poorhouse in Ayr, which (held by Ayrshire Archives) contain registers of inmates, financial records, punishment books and plans. Where a poorhouse became a hospital, records (including registers of inmates) may survive amongst the records of the hospital concerned, held by the appropriate health-board archive.

At The National Archives of Scotland the records of the Home and Health Department (under the reference HH) contain the minute books and other records of the Board of Supervision and the Local Government Board for Scotland, which supervised civil parishes in Scotland. These include annual reports and financial accounts of poorhouse committees.

Further details of Scotland's poorhouses, its Poor Laws and what records exist can be found on the Scottish Archive Network website at: www.scan.org.uk/knowledgebase/topics/poorhouses_topic.htm. Peter Higginbothan's workhouse website at: www.workhouses. org.uk/ also includes information on Scotland's Poor Laws and its poorhouses.

Poor Law unions

In the mid-nineteenth century Britain and Ireland were divided into Poor Law unions. These were created by amalgamating adjoining parishes and townships which also became registration districts for the purposes of registering births, marriages and deaths.

Most of the Poor Law unions were based upon market towns, and included the surrounding parishes which were serviced by their weekly market and other facilities. As the Poor Law Commissioners put it in their first annual report:

> The limits of unions which we have found most convenient are those of a circle, taking a market town as a centre, and comprehending those surrounding parishes whose inhabitants are accustomed to resort to the same market. This arrangement was found highly convenient for the weekly attendances of the parish officers, and some portion of the guardians. Some auxiliaries to good management were derived from the town itself.[1]

In 1851, 1861 and 1871 Poor Law union (or registration district) was the main geographical area used by the census authorities for the publication of their statistics. In 1861, for example, the information published at this level included the following tables: the numbers of males and females, the total population and the numbers of inhabited and uninhabited houses; the ages of males and females in five-year age groups; the numbers of boys and girls aged under 5; the marital condition of males and females broken down by age group; the occupations of males and females aged 20 and over; the birthplaces of males and females aged under 20, and aged 20 and over; the numbers of blind, deaf and dumb people; and the inmates of workhouses, prisons, lunatic asylums and hospitals.

A database listing over 12,000 English place names, the name of the Poor Law union it belonged to and the local record office holding records is available at: www.fourbears.worldonline.co.uk/html/union_finder_database.html. There is also a parish locator database of 25,000 parishes in England, Wales and Scotland at: web.onetel.net.uk/~gdlawson/parfind.htm. The family history website at: www.genuki.org.uk includes a number of links to sites listing Poor Law unions established in English and Welsh counties. Cambridgeshire's Poor Law unions, for example, can be found at: www.genuki.org.uk/big/eng/CAM/PoorLawUnions.html. A description of Ireland's Poor Law unions, together with a listing by county can be found at: www.askaboutireland.ie/show_topic.do?id=10.

Public Assistance Committees

The Local Government Act of 1929 abolished the Board of Guardians and placed the powers, duties, assets and liabilities of Poor Law unions with the county and civic boroughs. Local-authority Guardian Committees became responsible for poor-relief and, although certain closure periods may be in force, the A2A website can be searched for committee records that are held in county or metropolitan record offices.

Quarter Sessions

An ancestor would not need to be a law-breaker to appear in Quarter Session court records. Magistrates made decisions on everything from murder to the failure of a tradesman to display his name on the side of his cart. Many Poor Law cases found their way into the Quarter Sessions. Vagrants, incorrigible rogues, beggars and itinerant performers, such as jugglers, minstrels, fortune tellers and tricksters, could find themselves in court if they were unable to provide for themselves or their families. From the eighteenth century magistrates at Quarter Sessions also examined a pauper's right of settlement, heard appeals for payment of poor-relief, adjudicated on inter-parish disputes or a breach in a pauper's apprenticeship agreement. Quarter Session records, open to public inspection, can be found at The National Archives or local county and metropolitan record offices.

Ragged schools (see also Schools for the poor)

The National Archives at Kew hold records of many ragged schools, including minutes, registers and emigration information in series ED4, ED17, ED21 and ED49. Local county and metropolitan record offices also retain records of individual ragged schools. You can search for these on the A2A website.

Barnardo's retain an extensive photographic archive of ragged school pupils, dating back to 1866 when Thomas Barnardo started to photograph children in his care. Contact: Barnardo's Photographic and Film Archive, Tanners Lane, Barkingside, Ilford, Essex IG6 1QL. You can also visit the three Victorian canal-side warehouses, formerly used by Thomas Barnardo for his Copperfield Road Ragged School, which today houses the Ragged School Museum, with its recreated Victorian classroom. Contact: Ragged School Museum, 46–50 Copperfield Road, London E3 4RR (telephone: + 44 (0)208 980 6405; website:www. raggedschoolmuseum.org.uk/nextgen/).

Reformatories (see Industrial schools)

Removal orders (see also Settlement certificates)

Magistrates issued a removal order if they were satisfied a person or a family requesting (or were expected to request) poor-relief in a parish had no legal right of settlement there. The order directed the return to a parish where legal right of settlement existed. Those removed were escorted by a constable to the parish boundary. Magistrates also issued passes, recording the parish of legal settlement and required constables of parishes on the route to direct paupers through each parish until they reached their final destination. At that point the pauper might receive relief, but the receiving parish was entitled to deny liability and seek a further removal order. The courts gave a ruling where two parishes were in dispute and a summary of their adjudication may be held within the Quarter Session files. Where these and removal notices survive they will usually be held in the archives of local-authority record offices.

Schools for the poor (see also Ragged schools)

Prior to the eighteenth century there was no widespread provision for the schooling of the poor, the underprivileged and the broad masses of the labouring classes. Private fee-paying grammar schools reached only a small percentage of the population. It was widely believed that education should not be extended to the poor since it would upset the social order and increase expectations beyond acceptable levels. It was, however, desirable for the lower classes to be able to read the Bible for themselves, if only to help them understand they should accept their humble place in God's greater plan.

Charity schools, aimed at providing a basic education for the poor, became a prominent feature of eighteenth-century life; many were founded by the Society for Promoting Christian knowledge (SPCK). Others were founded by subscriptions or endowments. Today the SPCK continues its work as an Anglican mission agency, especially through the ministries of Christian education and literature. The Society's archives, which date from its foundation in 1698, are deposited with the Manuscripts Department at the University of Cambridge (contact: telephone: +44 (0)122 333 3143; website: www.lib.cam.ac.uk/deptserv/manuscripts/). Here can be found committee minutes, annual reports, details of legacies and grants,

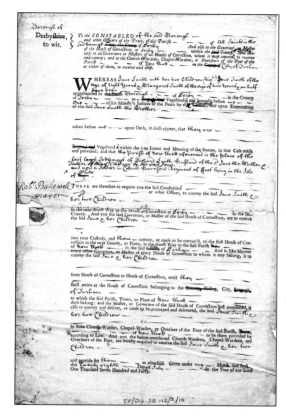

EP/Du.SO 112/2/10

A *removal notice issued to the constables instructing them to remove Jane Smith and her two children, Jane aged 8 years and Margaret aged 2½ years, from the parish of Derby. Her husband, and father of the children, Richard, was a soldier in Colonel Harrison's Regiment of Foot stationed on the Isle of Wight. Upon examination by magistrates the family were found to be vagrants and their place of legal settlement was New Elvott (Elvet) in the county of Durham. The document also authorises each house of correction (the forerunner to the workhouse) to accommodate the family on the route to their new parish.* (Reproduced by permission of Durham, St Oswald Parish and the Durham County Record Office (Ref: EP/Du.SO 112/2/10))

correspondence and information on its charity schools. The records of schools established by subscription or endowment exist today in the archives of local record offices identified by searching for school records on the A2A website.

Settlement certificates

Settlement certificates show relationships between family members and families and locations. A 'place of settlement' was the parish within which a person was entitled to receive assistance under the Poor Laws. There were very specific rules about how a settlement could be gained, and the Parliamentary Act of 1662 allowed for the removal (to a more appropriate parish) of anyone claiming poor-relief who did not have legal settlement there:

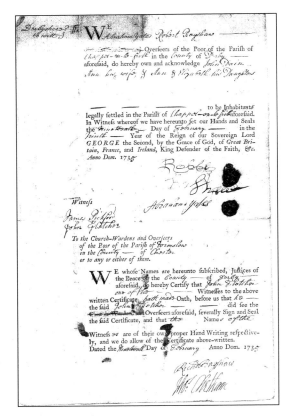

A settlement certificate issued by Abraham Gates and Robert Bradshaw, the Overseers of the Poor for the Parish of Chapel-en-le Firth, on 19 February 1735. This confirms that John Dain, his wife Elizabeth and their daughters Ann and Ann Elizabeth obtained legal right of settlement in the parish. (Reproduced by permission of Cheshire and Chester Archives and Local Studies (Ref: P123/2492/C3/2/1/40))

• A legitimate child took his father's settlement, which might not be the same as the child's place of birth;

• A wife took her husband's settlement;

• Children from the age of 7 could gain settlement in the parish where they were apprenticed, providing they lived there for more than forty consecutive days;

• A widow who remarried took her husband's settlement, but children from her first marriage retained their father's place of settlement;

• A married man who rented a farm, or was a tradesman in a new parish, providing he stayed for twelve months, paid parish rates and £10 or more in annual rent, could gain settlement there.

• Servants who stayed one year from the date of hiring could claim settlement in the parish where they were in service.

Settlement was determined by examination by magistrates or at Quarter Sessions, records of which should be found in local authority record offices. Early certificates may only mention a man's name and family, but later documents give much greater information on individuals and their families, often more than can be found on the early census returns. Parishioners would sometimes have a say in who got a certificate and it was not only paupers who requested settlement in a new parish. Craftsmen, tradesmen and labourers needed one too. Any persons not permitted to remain in their adopted parish were removed. Two magistrates signed a duplicate removal order and one copy would be given to each parish involved; their survival rate is therefore relatively good. Later orders can be particularly informative, giving reasons for removal and other family details, for example, where a woman was pregnant or a father in prison.

The laws of settlement were not formally abolished until 1948, but they gradually fell into disuse after 1834 when the Poor Law Amendment Act introduced Poor Law unions, the equalisation of poor-relief and reduced the need for people to move between neighbouring parishes.

Subscription charities (see Charity Commission)

Training ships

The Merseyside Museum (contact: telephone: +44 (0)151 478 4499; website: www.liverpoolmuseums.org.uk/maritime/archive/) holds annual reports, wage books and registers of boys on board training ships for various periods between 1859 and 1975. This includes the registers, minute books and general correspondence for the training ship *Indefatigable*. The admission registers for the reformatory ship *Clarence* are deposited at the Liverpool Record Office (contact: telephone: +44 (0)151 233 5817; website: www.liverpool.gov.uk /Leisure_and_culture/Libraries/Public_records/index.asp) and those of her sister ship *Akbar* are with the Lancashire Record Office (contact: telephone: +44 (0)177 253 3039; website: www.lancscc.gov.uk/ education/record_office/).

For detailed information on training ships used as reformatories, industrial, charity and naval training establishments, together with a list of record offices and other depositaries holding registers and minutes etc., see www.trainingships.royalnavy.co.uk/. The site also contains a number of links for researching and contacting sailors who were aboard Royal Navy training ships.

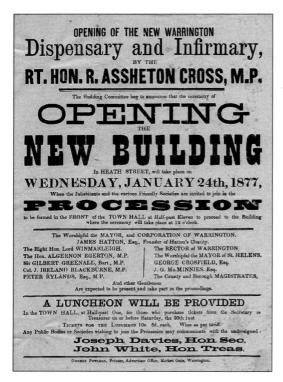

A poster advertising the opening of Warrington's new combined dispensary and infirmary building, funded in part by friendly societies, 1877. Complementing the work of voluntary hospitals were the dispensaries, which offered the working class an alternative, and sometimes only, means of obtaining medical treatment. Financed by voluntary contributions, the first dispensary was established by the Royal College of Physicians in 1697. But their growth was largely the result of the Industrial Revolution when voluntary hospitals failed to keep pace with health demands in new urban areas. (Reproduced by permission of Warrington Borough Council, Libraries, Heritage & Learning)

An interesting personal account by Gordon Sollors of life at The National Nautical School in Portishead from 1938 to 1942 is available at: www.geocities.com/trainingships/TrainingShips_ebook.htm.

There are a number of sites dedicated to sailors who served on training ships. The Association of Old Worcesters at: www.hms-worcester.co.uk/ and www.hmsconway.org/friends.html both contain detail histories, lists of officers and ratings, together with links to other sources of research.

Trust deeds

Trust deeds are the primary documents evidencing any permanent endowment to a charity, whether by endowment or gift. The deeds set out the aims and uses (the objects) of the endowment, how funds should be distributed, by whom and what happens if the charity ceases to exist. From 1736, to ensure the terms of any benefaction or gift were adequately provided for, trust deeds had to be formally drawn up and enrolled in the Court of Chancery and from 1903 in the Supreme Court Enrolment Books. These papers are now deposited with TNA under series C54 and J18 respectively. From 1856, any deed, will or other document relating to charities might also be enrolled in the books of the Charity Commission and held at Kew in series CHAR12. There is a useful research guide entitled 'Land Conveyances: Trust Deeds (Land for Charitable Uses), 1736–1925', available online from TNA at: www.nationalarchives.gov.uk.

Voluntary hospitals

The management, responsibility and records for voluntary hospitals passed to the National Health Service on 1 January 1948. Many hospital clinical records have been destroyed, although administrative records survive but are closed for thirty years. Patient records, including hospital admission registers, remain with the depositories collated in a hospital records database administered jointly by TNA and the Wellcome Trust. This searchable database catalogues the records of more than 1,000 hospitals and is available at: www.nationalarchives.gov.uk/hospitalrecords/. The Royal College of Nursing website at: www.rcn.org.uk/resources/historyofnursing/index.php includes information on the history of nursing, complete copies of the *Nursing Gazette* since 1888 and a fact sheet for family historians on tracing nursing ancestors. Records of many London hospitals are deposited with London Metropolitan Archives, details of which are available at: www.cityoflondon.gov.uk/Corporation/leisure_heritage/libraries_archives_museums_galleries/JAS/lma/records_held.htm.

Workhouse

Surviving records concerning the day-to-day administration of the workhouse can be found in county and metropolitan record offices. By the mid-nineteenth century the main types of registers of inmates had become standardised and include:
• Admission and discharge books. These are the daily lists of who was admitted, discharged or died;
• Registers of births. Until 1904 a birth certificate recorded the

workhouse as the place of birth. After this date the street occupied by the workhouse was used, often with euphemistic house names. London's Willesden Workhouse Infirmary, for example, became 'Twyford Lodge';

• Creed registers. These recorded, often in alphabetical order, the creed or faith of each inmate;

• Registers of deaths were also kept and in metropolitan areas the Poor Law authorities often entered into a contract with local authorities for burial of the poor;

• Records were also kept of inmates who were admitted to the workhouse infirmary or transferred to separate hospital for specialist care or treatment. These would include those who were sent to county lunatic asylums or in London, the Metropolitan Asylum Board hospitals.

A general online introduction to workhouse records and where they might be found is available at: www.workhouses.org.uk/ and www.institutions.org.uk/index.html.

Appendix 3

FURTHER READING

General works

Annal, David, *Easy Family History*, TNA, 2005
Briggs, Asa, *A Social History of England*, Viking Press, 1984
Bristow, Joy, *The Local Historian's Glossary of Words and Terms*, Countryside Books, 2001
Carter, Paul and Kate Thompson, *Sources for Local Historians*, Phillimore, 2005
Christian, Peter, *The Genealogist's Internet*, TNA, 2005
Herber, Mark, *Ancestral Trails*, Sutton Publishing, 2004
Kee, Robert, *Ireland – A History*, Abacus, 2003
Raymond, Stuart, *Family History on the Web: an Internet Directory for England and Wales*, Federation of Family History Societies, 2001
Raymond, Stuart, *Scottish Family History on the Web*, Federation of Family History Societies, 2002
Raymond, Stuart, *Irish Family History on the Web*, Federation of Family History Societies, 2004
Richardson, John, *The Local Historian's Encyclopaedia*, Historical Publications, 2003
Yaxley, David, *A Researcher's Glossary: Of Words Found in Historical Documents of East Anglia*, The Larks Press, 2003

Poverty related works

Alvey, Norman, *From Chantry to Oxfam*, Phillimore, 1995
Anderson, Janice, *The War Years: Life in Britain During 1939–1945*, Futura, 2007
Bailey, Brian, *Almshouses*, Robert Hale, 1988
Beckett, Ian, *Home Front 1914–1918: How Britain survived the War Years*, TNA, 2006
Booth, Frank, *Robert Raikes of Gloucester*, National Christian Education

Council, 1980

Cole, Anne, *Poor Law Documents before 1834*, Federation of Family History Societies, 1993

Corbett, Gail, *Nation Builders*, Dundurn Press, 1997

Cordery, Simon, *British Friendly Societies 1750–1914*, Palgrave Macmillan, 2003

Davin, Anna, *Growing Up Poor: Home, School and Street in London, 1870–1914*, Rivers Oram Press, 1995

Dyer, Christopher, *Standards of Living in the Later Middle Ages*, Cambridge University Press, 1989

Dyer, Christopher, *Everyday Life in Medieval England*, Hambledown Press, 1994

Engels, Frederick, *The Condition of the Working Class in England*, Hard Press, 2006

Englander, David, *Poverty and Poor Law Reform in Nineteenth Century Britain, 1834–1914: From Chadwick to Booth*, Longman, 1998

Fowler, Simon, *Workhouse: The People, the Places, the Life Behind Doors*, TNA, 2008

Fraser, Derek, *The Evolution of the British Welfare State*, Palgrave Macmillan, 2002

Gibson, Jeremy and Colin Rogers, *Poor Law Union Records, Federation of Family History Societies*, 1993/97

Glennerster, Howard, John Hills, David Piachaud and Jo Webb, *One hundred years of poverty and policy*, Joseph Rowntree Foundation, 2004

Hammond, J L and Barbara, *The Village Labourer 1760–1832: A Study in the Government of England before the Reform Bill*, first published 1911 and available online at: www.socserv.mcmaster.ca/econ/ugcm/3113 /hammond/village.html

Hey, David, *How our Ancestors lived*, Public Record Office, 2002

Howson, Brian, *Houses of Noble Poverty: A History of English Almshouses*, Bellevue Books, 1993

Jordan, W K, *Philanthropy in England 1480–1660*, George Allen & Unwin, 1959

Kelly, John, *The Great Mortality – An Intimate History of the Black Death*, Fourth Estate, 2005

Kershaw, Roger and Mark Pearsall, *Family History on the Move*, TNA, 2006

Kershaw, Roger and Janet Sacks, *New lives for Old*, TNA, 2008

Lavalette, Michael, *A Thing of the Past? – Child Labour in Britain in the Nineteenth and Twentieth Centuries*, Liverpool University Press, 1999

Logan, Roger, *An Introduction to Friendly Society Records*, Federation of Family History Societies, 2000

Longmate, Norman, *The Workhouse*, Pimlico, 2003

Mitchison, Rosalind, *The Old Poor Law in Scotland – the Experience of Poverty, 1574–1845*, Edinburgh University Press, 2000

Murray, Peter, *Poverty & Welfare 1830–1914*, Hodder & Stoughton, 1999

O'Day, Rosemary and David Englander, *Mr Charles Booth's Inquiry: Life and Labour of the People in London Reconsidered*, Hambledon Continuum, 1993

Pound, John, *Poverty and Vagrancy in Tudor England*, Longman, 1986

Rimmer, Joan, *Yesterday's Naughty Children*, Neil Richardson, 1986

Royle, Edward, *Modern Britain: A Social History 1750–1997*, Hodder Arnold, 1997

Ryan, James, *Irish Records: Sources for Family and Local History*, Flyleaf Press, 1997

Seymour, Claire, *Ragged Schools, Ragged Children*, Ragged School Museum Trust, 1995

Shuter, Jane, *Poor in Tudor England*, Heinemann Educational Books, 1995

Slack, Paul, *Poverty and Policy in Tudor and Stuart England*, Longman, 1988

Slack, Paul, *The English Poor Law*, Cambridge University Press, 1990

Tate, W E, *The Parish Chest*, Phillimore, 1983

Thane, Pat, *Foundations of the Welfare State*, Longman, 1996

Thompson, Flora, *Lark Rise to Candleford*, Century Publishing, 1983

Timmins, Nicholas, *The Five Giants – A Biography of the Welfare State*, Harper Collins, 1995

Tompson, Richard, *The Charity Commission and the Age of Reform*, Routledge and Kegan Paul, 1979

Wagner, Gillian, *Barnardo*, Weidenfeld and Nicolson, 1979

Waller, John, *The Real Oliver Twist: Robert Blincoe – A Life That Illuminates an Age*, Icon Books, 2005

Woodham Smith, Cecil, *The Great Hunger: Ireland 1845–1849*, Penguin Books, 1991

Woodward, John, *To Do the Sick No Harm – A Study of the British Voluntary Hospital System to 1875*, Routledge and Kegan Paul, 1974

Appendix 4

USEFUL WEBSITES

This appendix lists some of the general 'getting started' websites for family historians together with those devoted to aspects of poverty, either by topic or which are regional in their coverage. Websites are also listed, where appropriate, in the Records Section (Appendix 2). The prefix http:// should be added to all website addresses identified in this book. A further selection of sites is listed in Peter Christian's *The Genealogist's Internet* (TNA, 2005). See also Stuart Raymond's trilogy of books: *Family History on the Web: an Internet Directory for England and Wales* (Federation of Family History Societies, 2001); *Scottish Family History on the Web* (Federation of Family History Societies, 2002); and *Irish Family History on the Web* (Federation of Family History Societies, 2004).

Access to Archives (A2A): www.nationalarchives.gov.uk/a2a/
Archives Network Wales: www.archivesnetworkwales.info/
ARCHON Directory of local, metropolitan and national record offices: www.nationalarchives.gov.uk/archon/
BBC Family History: www.bbc.co.uk/familyhistory/
Census Records (England and Wales): www.nationalarchives.gov.uk/census/default.htm?homepage=fr-census
Census Records (Ireland): www.nationalarchives.ie/genealogy/censusrtns.html
Census Records (Scotland): www.scotlandspeople.gov.uk/
Charity Commission for England and Wales: www.charity-commission.gov.uk
Federation of Family History Societies: www.ffhs.org.uk
FFHS publications and online bookshop: www.genfair.co.uk
'Gateway' family history website: www.cyndislist.com/ and GENUKI: www.genuki.org.uk/
General Register Office (England and Wales) for birth, marriage and death certificates: www.gro.gov.uk/gro/content/

General Register Office for Scotland: www.gro-scotland.gov.uk/
General Registry Office (Ireland): www.groireland.ie/
Guide to the workhouses of Britain and Ireland with historical notes, maps, photographs and much more: www.workhouses.org.uk/
Local, national and regional study centres – contact details and location: www.familia.org.uk
National Archives of Australia: www.naa/gov.au
National Archives of Canada: www.archives.ca
National Archives of Ireland: www.nationalarchives.ie
National Archives of Scotland: www.nas.gov.uk
The National Archives of the United Kingdom: www.national archives.gov.uk
Office of the Scottish Charity Regulator: www.oscr.org.uk/
Rossbret Institution: www.institutions.org.uk/index
Scottish Archive Network: www.scan.org.uk/
Society of Genealogists: www.sog.org.uk/index.shtml

Appendix 5

NOTES AND REFERENCES

Preface

1. *British Social Attitudes: the 24th Report* (National Centre for Social Research, 2008).

Introduction

1. Seebolm Rowntree, *Poverty: A Study of Town Life* (Macmillan & Co., 1901), p. 120.
2. Edward Royle, *Modern Britain: A Social History 1750–1997* (Hodder Arnold, 1997), p. 187.

Chapter 1: The Causes of Poverty in Pre-industrial Britain

1. The *Anglo Saxon Chronicles* can be read online at: www.webmesh. co.uk/a-s-homepage.htm.
2. John Kelly, *The Great Mortality – An Intimate History of the Black Death* (Fourth Estate, 2005), p. 59.
3. Asa Briggs, *A Social History of England* (Viking Press, 1984), p. 83.
4. Kelly, *The Great Mortality*, p. 62.
5. John Pound, *Poverty and Vagrancy in Tudor England* (Longman, 1986), p. 3.
6. Act Against the Decaying of Towns and Houses of Husbandry, 1598.
7. Act for the Maintenance of Husbandry and Tillage, 1598.
8. W K Jordan, *Philanthropy in England 1480–1660* (George Allen & Unwin, 1959), p. 96.
9. Ibid., p. 69.
10. Ibid., p. 70.
11. Pound, *Poverty and Vagrancy*, p. 14.

Chapter 2: The Causes of Poverty in the Industrial Age

1. Frederick Engels, *The Condition of the Working Class in England* (George Allen & Unwin, 1844), pp. 97–99, 123–126.
2. Ibid.
3. Royle, *Modern Britain*, p. 165.
4. Robert Kee, *Ireland – A History* (2003), pp. 77–101.
5. Ibid.
6. Cecil Woodham Smith, *The Great Hunger: Ireland 1845–1849*, (Penguin Books, 1991), p. 56.
7. First Report of the Registrar General, 1839.
8. David Owen, *English Philanthropy 1660–1960* (Harvard University Press, 1965), p. 135.
9. Andrew Mearns, *The Bitter Cry of Outcast London* (Leicester University Press, 1970).
10. Charles Booth, *Life and Labour of the People of London* (Macmillan & Co., 1889–1903).
11. William Booth, *In Darkest England and the Way Out* (Funk and Wagnall, 1890).
12. Booth, *Life and Labour*, Vol. I, *East, Central and South London* (1892), p. 99.
13. Ibid.
14. Seebolm Rowntree, *The Human Needs of Nature* (Macmillan & Co., 1918).
15. B S Rowntree and M Kendal, *How the Labourer Lives: A Study of Rural Labour Problem* (1913), pp. 31–32, quoted from Royle, *Modern Britain*, p. 165.

Chapter 3: Early State Intervention

1. Act Concerning Punishment of Beggars and Vagabonds, 1531.
2. Punishment of Beggars and Vagabonds Act, 1531.
3. Act for the Punishment of Sturdy Vagabonds and Beggars, 1536.
4. Jordan, *Philanthropy in England*, p. 85.
5. Punishment of Vagabonds and the Relief of the Poor and Impotent Persons Act, 1547.
6. Provision and Relief of the Poor Act, 1551.
7. Ibid.
8. Quoted from TNA 'learning curve' website: www.learningcurve. gov.uk/tudorhackney/localhistory/lochlg.asp.

9. Punishment of Vagabonds and for the Relief of the Poor and Impotent Act, 1572.
10. Ibid.
11. Jordan, *Philanthropy in England*, p. 88.
12. Frank Aydelotte, *Elizabethan Rogues and Vagabonds* (1913), quoted from Pound, *Poverty and Vagrancy*, p. 45.
13. Act for the Setting the Poor on Work, 1576.
14. Pound, *Poverty and Vagrancy*, p. 50.
15. Act for the Relief of the Poor, 1598.
16. Cornwall Record Office, Ref: B/MZ/11/1/6.
17. Act for the Relief of the Poor, 1598.
18. Act for supplying the Defects of the former Laws for the Settlement of the Poor, 1697.
19. Cornwall Record Office, Ref: B/MZ/11/6/12.
20. Cornwall Record Office, Ref: B/MZ/11/6/22.
21. Rogues, Vagabonds and other Idle and Disorderly Persons Act, 1744.
22. Amending the Laws relating to the Settlement, Employment and Relief of the Poor' (the 'Workhouse Test Act')], 1723.
23. Quoted from Norman Longmate, *The Workhouse* (Pimlico, 2003), p. 24.
24. Ibid.
25. Quoted from Peter Higginbotham's website at: www.workhouses. org.uk/.
26. Ibid.
27. Act for the Better Relief and Employment of the Poor, 1782.
28. [Act] Of thiggaris = about beggars, from the verb thig, to beg; and thiggar, meaning beggar (19 James I c.21).
29. [Act] for the stanching of Maisterfull Beggaris with addition = for the restraining of masterful and strong beggars. (text of the Act refers to 'the multitude of maisterfull and strang beggaris') (23 James I c.29).
30. [Act] for the punishment of the strang and ydle beggaris & and relief of the pure [poor] & impotent = for the punishment of the strong and idle (or lazy) beggars and the relief of the poor and weak (or feeble) (13 James VI c.12).
31. Strang Beggaris, Vagabondis & Egiptians suld be punished = strong beggars, vagrants and Gypsies should be punished (31 James VI c39).
32. Act for establishing Correction-houses for Idle beggars &

vagabonds = Act to establish houses of correction for idle (or lazy) beggars and vagrants (13 Charles II c42).

Chapter 4: Charity in Pre-industrial Britain

1. The seven Corporeal Works of Mercy – to feed the hungry; give drink to the thirsty; welcome the stranger; clothe the naked; visit the sick; visit the prisoner; and bury the dead – were promulgated in AD 816 at the Catholic Synod at Aix-la-Chapelle in France.
2. Christopher Dyer, *Standards of Living in the Later Middle Ages* (Cambridge University Press, 1989), p. 238.
3. Ibid., p. 237.
4. B Kirkman Gray, *A History of English Philanthropy* (Frank Cass, new impression 1967), p. 10.
5. Brian Howson, *Houses of Noble Poverty – A History of the English Almshouse* (Bellevue Books, 1993), p. 57.
6. Pound, *Poverty and Vagrancy*, p. 73.
7. Howson, *Houses of Noble Poverty*, p. 54.
8. Paul Slack, *Poverty and Policy in Tudor and Stuart England* (Longman, 1988), p. 13.
9. John Woodward, *To Do the Sick No Harm – A Study of the British Voluntary Hospital System to 1875* (Routledge and Kegan Paul, 1974), p. 2.
10. Jordan, *Philanthropy in England*, p. 246.
11. Quoted from Owen, *English Philanthropy*, p. 2.
12. Jordan, *Philanthropy in England*, p. 369.
13. Ibid., p. 256.
14. Kirkman Gray, *A History of English Philanthropy*, p. 4.
15. Pound, *Poverty and Vagrancy*, p. 73.
16. Slack, *Poverty and Policy*, p. 167.
17. Norman Alvey, *From Chantry to Oxfam* (Phillimore, 1995), p. 15.
18. Ibid., p. 23.

Chapter 5: Poor Laws in the Nineteenth Century

1. Report of the Poor Law Commission, 1834.
2. Act for the Regulation of Parish Vestries and the Act to Amend the Laws for the Relief of the Poor.
3. Thomas Malthus, *Essay on Population* (1796).
4. Report of the Poor Law Commission, 1834.

5. Peter Murray, *Poverty & Welfare 1830–1914* (Hodder & Stoughton, 1999), p. 24.
6. Report of the Poor Law Commission, 1834.
7. Ibid.
8. Ibid.
9. Ibid.
10. Ibid.
11. Ibid.
12. Murray, *Poverty & Welfare*, p. 53.
13. Mark Heber, *Ancestral Trials* (Sutton Publishing, 2004), p. 736.
14. Editorial from *The Times*, 30 January 1837.
15. Ibid.
16. Royle, *Modern Britain*, p. 183.
17. The *Lancet*, April 1865.
18. Ibid.
19. Murray, *Poverty & Welfare*, p. 49.
20. Quoted from Murray, *Poverty & Welfare*, p. 49.
21. Royle, *Modern Britain*, p. 184.

Chapter 6: Charity and Self-help in the Industrial Age

1. Richard Tompson, *The Charity Commission and the Age of Reform* (Routledge and Kegan Paul, 1979), p. 79.
2. Ibid.
3. Ibid., p. 94.
4. Royle, *Modern Britain*, p. 187.
5. Thomas De Laune, *Angliae Metropolis – the present state of London*, p. 156, quoted from Woodward, *To Do the Sick No Harm*, p. 3.
6. Murray, *Poverty & Welfare*, p. 63.
7. Quoted from the Wrington History website at: www.wrington somerset.org.uk/.
8. Lynn Lees, *Exiles of Erin* (Manchester University Press, 1979), p. 83.
9. George Sims, *How the Poor Live, and Horrible London* (s.n., 1899).
10. Report of the Committee on the Law and Practice relating to Charitable Trusts, 1952 (Nathan Report).

Chapter 7: The Welfare State

1. *Ancestors* magazine, January 2007 (issue 53).
2. Report of the Poor Law Commission, quoted from *The Times*,

18 February 1909, p. 13.

3. Ibid., p. 48.

4. Helen Bosanquet, *The Poor Law Report of 1909* (Macmillan, 1909), p. 272.

5. Murray, *Poverty & Welfare*, p. 105.

6. Report from the Select Committee on Home Work (HMSO, 1907), p. 6.

7. Murray, *Poverty & Welfare*, p. 108.

8. Flora Thompson, *The Illustrated Lark Rise to Candleford* (Century Publishing, 1983), p. 191.

9. Pat Thane, *Foundations of the Welfare State* (Longman, 1996), p. 83.

10. Royle, *Modern Britain*, p. 177.

11. Briggs, *A Social History of England*, p. 284.

12. Arthur Marwick, *Total War and Social Change* (Palgrave Macmillan 1988), p. 235.

13. Briggs, *A Social History of England*, p. 284.

14. Ibid.

Chapter 8: Destitute Children – a Case Study

1. Interview from the *Ashton Times*, 1849.

2. Matthew Arnold, *Culture of Anarchy* (Smith, Elder and Co., 1869), p. 48.

3. Charles Dickens, *Oliver Twist* (s.n., 1838).

4. C J Montague, *Sixty Years of Waifdom* (Charles Murray, 1904).

5. Report from the Select Committee on Criminal and Destitute Juveniles (1852), p. 156.

6. Claire Seymour, *Ragged Schools, Ragged Children* (Ragged School Museum Trust, 1995), p. 7.

7. Report from the Select Committee on Criminal and Destitute Juveniles, p. 158.

8. Gillian Wagner, *Barnardo* (Weidenfeld and Nicolson, 1979), p. 42.

9. Henry Mayhew, *London Labour and the London Poor* (Charles Griffin, 1861), p. 59.

10. Philip Bean and Joy Melville, *Lost Children of the Empire* (Unwin Hyman Ltd, 1989), p. 33.

11. Quoted from the Devon County Council website at: www. devon.gov.uk/index/ democracycommunities/neighbourhoods-villages/record_office/family_history_3/school_records/industria l_schools.htm#exeter_girls.

12. Report from the Select Committee on Criminal and Destitute Juveniles, p. 145.
13. Montague, *Sixty Years of Waifdom*, p. 39.
14. Wagner, *Barnardo*, p. 281.
15. Bean and Melville, *Lost Children of the Empire*, p. 51.
16. Ibid., p. 80.
17. Gillian Wagner, *Children of the Empire* (Unwin Hyman Ltd, 1982), p. 57.
18. Bean and Melville, *Lost Children of the Empire*, p. 43.
19. Ibid., p. 118.
20. Ibid., p. 45.

Appendix 1: Getting Started

1. Charles Shaw, *When I was a Child* (Caliban Books, 1977), p. 96.
2. Quoted from the Greater Manchester County Record Office website at: www.gmcro.co.uk/cs/starting_out.htm.

Appendix 2: The Records

1. First Annual Report of the Poor Law Commissioners with Appendices (HMSO, 1835), p. 19.

INDEX